Emily .... te

Also in this series

Emily Post on Invitations and Letters

Emily Post on Entertaining

Emily Post on Etiquette

Emily Post on Weddings

EMILY POST on Business Etiquette

Elizabeth L. Post

Harper & Row, Publishers, New York
Grand Rapids, Philadelphia, St. Louis, San Francisco
London, Singapore, Sydney, Tokyo, Toronto

EMILY POST ON BUSINESS ETIQUETTE. Copyright © 1990 by Elizabeth L. Post. All rights reserved. Printed in the United States of America. No part of this book may be used or reproduced in any manner whatsoever without written permission except in the case of brief quotations embodied in critical articles and reviews. For information address Harper & Row, Publishers, Inc., 10 East 53rd Street, New York, NY 10022.

FIRST EDITION

Designed by Kim Llewellyn

ISBN 0-06-081036-X

Contents

Introduction

As we travel today from living room to board room, we take our manners with us. If we were raised to jump to our feet when an older woman entered the room, our instinct is to do the same when a senior woman executive enters a meeting. As polite as that may seem, it may not be the appropriate thing to do. If a young boy was taught to remove his hat whenever he entered a building or an elevator, he more than likely does the same thing, all grown up, when arriving at his office. Should he? Business etiquette has a set of rules all its own, and this book is designed to explain those rules, based on many of the most often-asked questions I have received.

It is also based on the premise that the golden rules in business are that people help each other when help is needed; that people respect one another across all levels, treating one another with courtesy and thoughtfulness; and that business etiquette rules are basically the same for women as they are for men.

These golden rules mean that some traditions need to be set aside as gender is set aside, and that some need to be maintained, contingent upon the situation. For example, all men seated in a meeting do not leap up when a woman enters the room. It would be disruptive to the meeting, and her gender is not at issue, as it would be outside the office. On the other hand, European businessmen tend to carry their chivalrous tendencies and social manners with them through the business day. To refuse their instincts would be rude. This, then, is a case where traditions need to be temporarily maintained.

Additionally, new technology and instant communication bring with them their own guidelines for professional and correct behavior. Supervisors find they have happier and more productive employees when courtesy and manners are practiced, and coworkers find greater cooperation when they employ the essence of etiquette to their everyday work life.

Succeeding in business today requires not only mastery of one's job but also mastery of the common courtesies of give and take and of consideration for others. Not only does this make the office a pleasanter place to be, it helps you leave a favorable impression behind, whatever you do. Whether you are making a first impression during a job interview or representing your company to others, your manners are often counted as highly as your knowledge of your subject matter or your brilliance in the conference room. Put them to work today, and you will find that they will work for you in all your professional days to come.

Elizabeth L. Post
May 1990

Emily Post on Business Etiquette

Interview and New Job Etiquette

Q. *How do I know how to dress for a job interview?*
A. What you wear depends on the type of job for which you are interviewing, combined with common sense. For example, even though you may be going on an interview for a job as a tennis pro, you would not wear your whites and carry a racket. A man would wear a business suit or a sport coat and slacks, a shirt, and a tie, and a woman would wear a daytime dress or coordinated suit or jacket and skirt. A man interviewing for a corporate position would wear a business suit; a woman applying for the same job would again wear a daytime dress or business coordinates.

Your appearance is the first factor an interviewer notices about you, so it should be as favorable and professional as possible. The most important factors are neatness, cleanliness, and appropriateness. Excessive jewelry or makeup and elaborate, dressy, sheer, or tight clothing are not appropriate. Grooming should be immaculate, with hair and nails clean. Buttons should not be missing; hems and cuffs should not be frayed or raveling. Shoes should be clean and shined, and should not be run down at the heel.

Q. *I'm anxious to show how much I want this job. How much ahead of time should I arrive for the appointment?*

A. One should not be more than ten minutes early for an appointment. "Camping out" in someone's reception area for an extended period of time can be an annoyance and will win you no points. Promptness is very important; being extremely early is no better than being a little late, which is equally as annoying. If you do arrive ten minutes early, ask where the washroom is and quickly check your appearance.

Q. *When beginning an interview, do I sit down upon entering the office or wait to be asked to be seated?*

A. You wait to be asked. If a specific chair is indicated for you, be seated there. If, however, the chair is not comfortable or you find yourself squinting into a window or bright light, it is perfectly all right to say, "That light is shining directly into my eyes and making it difficult for me to see you. If you don't mind, I'm going to change to that chair."

If no particular chair is indicated, select one that positions you across from the interviewer to enable you to maintain eye contact and to talk without having to twist around in your chair.

Q. *On my last interview, the interviewer asked me several personal and seemingly unrelated questions which I found quite offensive. How should I handle that if it happens again?*

A. By law, interviewers are not allowed to ask you your race or religion. Other questions, such as those about your personal finances, your credit rating, or your home life, for example, are not appropriate unless you are being interviewed for a job which requires extensive security clearance. If you feel you are being asked questions that are too personal in nature, respond by saying, "Why do you ask?" If the answer you receive is not acceptable, don't say, "What a rude question"; but you may reply that you do not understand what the questions have to do with the job being offered and would prefer to delay discussing your personal life until both of you have determined a mutual interest in your candidacy for the position.

Q. *Are there any things not to do on an interview because they are ill-mannered?*
A. Of course, just as in social situations. Do not chew gum; do not smoke unless invited to do so; do not slouch (which indicates lack of interest); do not ask for refreshment (unless you are coughing and need a glass of water to recompose yourself); do not fiddle, tap or bounce; and do not monopolize the conversation with endless personal narrative. Do have a firm handshake, listen and maintain eye contact both when speaking and when listening.

Q. *After I left my last interview, I thought of a few more questions. Would it be all right to call and ask them, or should I wait to hear from the company?*
A. Unless the interviewer suggested that you call if you thought of additional questions, it is preferable that you wait to hear from him or her. You have no real grounds for needing to know additional answers

until the company has indicated an interest in you. Write your questions down. In the event that you receive the call, you will be prepared, and your queries will indicate that you have thought about the job and that you are interested. Do not include them in your thank you note; this note should be a brief statement of appreciation for the time the interviewer spent with you not a lengthy questionnaire which indicates that you expect answers to questions which should have been discussed during the interview.

Q. *I think the interview went well. How soon after the interview is it appropriate to call the personnel office and find out if a decision has been made?*

A. First, you should write a thank-you note to the person who interviewed you. Not only is this good manners, but it helps the interviewer keep you in mind when he or she is making a decision as to whom to hire. You should give the thank-you note at least three days to arrive before calling to find out if a decision has been made. When you do call, if you are told that a decision has not been made, you may ask if interviews for the job are still being conducted and also ask that you be notified, even if the decision is a negative one. In the future, it is appropriate to ask, at the end of your interview, when it is expected that a decision will be made (so that you have a time frame to use for a follow-up telephone call).

Q. *I'm being recruited by several companies and wined and dined as part of the process. Do I send thank-you notes to the recruiters?*

A. Yes, it is appropriate to send a thank-you note, even if you are not interested at the moment in the company or the job. It is good manners, and it leaves a favorable impression about you, your courtesy, and your ability to follow through.

Q. *After I've accepted a position, should I write thank-you notes to those corporations I turned down?*
A. You don't have to, but it is a good idea. You may want to work for that company someday, and a thank-you note now leaves an especially good impression for the future.

Your letter should be directed to the person whose final decision it was to offer you the job. It should express your thanks for the offer and again for the time he or she spent with you (even though you have already sent a thank-you note following your interview) and should explain that you have accepted another position. You should not go into detail about the job you have accepted or justify your decision, nor do you have to name the company you will be working for, although you may.

Q. *I'm starting a new job and do not know how to address the people I will be working with and for. Is it proper to call them by their first names?*
A. Always call your boss "Mrs. Knowles" or "Mr. Andrews" until asked to use his or her first name. Take your cue whether it is appropriate to call other people by their first names at the time you are introduced and by listening to co-workers as they address one another. It is much safer to use "Mr.," "Mrs.,"

"Ms" or "Miss" than to assume it is all right to use first names. If, in response, someone says "Oh, please call me Susan," then by all means do so. If you can get no indication as to what is accepted, then ask. Ask your supervisor, the person who is introducing you, or someone in the personnel department.

Q. *During my first few days on my new job, no one asked me to have lunch. Would it have been all right for me to ask if I could join them? I didn't, and while they eventually began including me, I would have liked someone to talk to at the beginning.*
A. It was better that you waited and didn't appear to be forcing yourself on others in the office. As the new person, you are in a position of not knowing what relationships exist, what arrangements are customary, or how friendly others in the office are. By giving them a chance to get to know you a little through work and giving yourself a chance to discreetly observe what lunchtime custom is, you did not put yourself in an awkward position. This is not to say that someone should not have included you immediately, but since no one did, manners dictate that the new kid on the block waits to be invited.

Q. *When I started my new job, I didn't have a lot of basic equipment like a stapler or paper clips. I asked the person at the next desk if I could use her stapler and borrow a few other items, and she seemed offended. What should I have done?*
A. You did nothing wrong in asking to borrow, but it is probably better to assess your needs, make a list

of what is missing, and ask the office manager or your boss how you should go about ordering or obtaining the items you feel you need. If your order will take a few days to fill, search for the friendliest person from whom to borrow and promise to replace the items when your order comes in. Some offices keep close tabs on such things as pens and pencils, and a negative reaction could be because the person from whom you try to borrow is afraid of running out or being accused of excess. Your promise to replace the borrowed items, whether this is the case or not, alleviates this anxiety.

Q. *When I was interviewed for the job I am about to begin, I noticed that there was a coffee pot and pastry in the workroom. Should I bring my own coffee the first day or figure that the coffee there is for everyone?*
A. The first day, bring your own and then ask. Inquire as to whether the coffee is for everyone, whether you may join in and chip in or not. It would not be good form to arrive the first day, stroll to the coffee pot, and pour yourself a cup without knowing what the arrangement is.

Q. *Are there any rules about personal telephone calls in the office? I am about to start a new job and always call my children after school to make sure they are home safely; but it will be a toll call, and I don't know what to do.*
A. Personal calls should always be kept to a minimum in the office, whether you are a long-time employee or a brand new one, a top executive or her secretary.

Since you need to know that your children are all right, ask them to call you when they get home so the charge for the call is yours, not the company's. When they do call, keep your time talking to them brief.

Q. *Who do you say hello to in the morning and good-night to at the end of the day?*
A. You address those people you see in passing on the way to your desk, whether they be the elevator operator or the president of the company. Not to greet them would seem churlish and ill mannered. You also would greet or say good-night to those people in the vicinity of your work area and, naturally, those who speak to you. You do not spend several minutes strolling through the floor or department greeting everyone, however, as though you were the hospitality chairperson.

Q. *I work for a large corporation. In the morning I often find myself arriving the same time as the company president and riding in the elevator with her. I never know if I should say hello and make small talk or wait for her to say something first.*
A. If you are the only two people in the elevator, you would naturally say "Good morning," and you may make a comment about the weather or ask "How are you this morning?" If she is unresponsive or cool in her reply, then simply say "Good morning" in the future, since it would be awkward not to, but do not engage in conversation. This is never the appropriate time to make comments about business or the company, since she is captive and could resent your intru-

sion. If one or two other people are in the elevator with you, you may still smile and say "Good morning," but do not continue to chat. If the elevator is crowded and no one is speaking, then neither should you, although it is appropriate to nod, smile, or reply if she greets you or to say "Good morning" if you make eye contact.

Q. *One of my associates always replies to the president of our company by saying "Yes, sir" or "No, sir." What do you think of this?*

A. Unless you work in a branch of the military, are of high school age, or work for the President of the United States or royalty, the use of "sir" and "ma'am" in the office is no longer necessary and actually sounds obsequious. It is entirely professional and much friendlier to say "Yes, Mr. Adams" or "No, Jim" (if your company is on a first-name basis) than to "sir" and "ma'am" superiors.

Communications
at Work

Q. *How do I address a letter when I don't know whether the person is a woman or a man?*
A. If you are able, call the person's office and ask the receptionist or secretary. If not, you may use the person's first and last names in the salutation ("Dear Sean Amdur") or you may write "Dear Sir or Madam."

Q. *How should one answer a business telephone?*
A. If answering your own telephone, standard business practice is to say "Hello, Jane Mittler," simply "Jane Mittler," or "Jane Mittler speaking."

If answering someone else's telephone, "Hello, Miss Mittler's office" or "Miss Mittler's office, may I help you?" are both courteous and efficient.

If the telephone being answered is a general number to a department, the usual way to answer is to say "Hello, Editorial Department" or "Editorial Department, may I help you?" Identifying the telephone being answered saves time both for you and the caller, eliminating the necessity of the caller first asking "Is this Miss Mittler's office?" or "Have I reached the editorial department?"

Central or switchboard operators should answer

with the name of the organization or company, saying "Consolidated General, good morning."

Q. *I have an 800 number at my office. My friends have started calling me on that number since they don't have to pay for the call. Is this all right?*
A. Absolutely not. Your company engaged that system for the convenience of clients and pays for every call that comes in on that number. It is not only ill-mannered to tie it up on personal calls but unethical to be charging the company for your personal business. Gently tell your friends that, as much as you love hearing from them, they have to discontinue using that number to reach you.

Q. *Part of my job is taking phone messages. My boss instructed me to find out what the call is about. How do I politely respond to callers who refuse to leave a message beyond "Please call"?*
A. When you have asked them to relay the nature of the message to you and they have refused, you may firmly say "I am sorry, but Mr. Johannson does not speak with people unknown to him until he is aware of the purpose of their call" or "Mr. Johannson has asked that I always relay to him the nature of a call before he will return it. If you would please give me your message, I will be sure he receives it so that he or someone else who can be of assistance can call you back." If the caller insists that his or her call is personal, then you should not be expected to persist in requesting a message, and the note you leave for your boss just indicates that it is a personal call.

Q. *What are the ingredients of a good phone message?*
A. In addition to neatness, accuracy, and legibility, a good phone message should include the date and time of the call; the caller's name and company, if any; the caller's telephone number; the message; and your signature or initials so the person for whom you have written the message knows whom to ask for any additional information.

Q. *I'm a receptionist. My job is taking phone messages. When I ask callers to leave their number, many say "She'll know." Is there a polite way to get these callers to leave their phone number?*
A. Say "I'm sure she will, but I have been asked to always include a telephone number with a message to facilitate your call being returned as soon as possible." If someone absolutely refuses to leave a number after you have said this, then make sure the message you leave states "Refused to leave telephone number."

Q. *Is there a correct way to talk to an answering machine?*
A. Yes, there is. Since many machines have a built-in time limit for messages, it is important to be succinct. First identify yourself. Don't assume someone will recognize your voice. If the recorded message asks you to state the day and time of your call, do so. If you are leaving a message, give the message, with all pertinent information. If you are asking for your call to be returned, give your telephone number and the best time to reach you, and add the reason for your call, briefly, so that the person returning it is prepared to

discuss the topic when calling. If you are requesting information that you need by a certain time, include your deadline ("I need to know your answer by tomorrow morning for an 11 A.M. meeting").

Q. *Answering machines are built into many business telephone systems these days, but I prefer to talk to a human being. Should I just hang up?*
A. You certainly may hang up, but it is likely in many instances that you will not reach a human without "talking" to a machine first. Many machines, designed to work with a touch tone telephone, automatically and ultimately connect you to a human voice after asking you to respond, with the push of button, to a series of questions. These machines take the place of a main switchboard operator and usually connect you directly to the telephone line of the person who will help you with your question. In other offices, answering machines have become a way of business today and are used regularly to receive messages. Many executives find their use increases efficiency and enables them to set aside specific times for returning calls instead of being interrupted throughout the day. When this is the case, you have a much better chance of getting your call through if you leave your name, telephone number, and message than if you hang up and redial at intervals, hoping to hear a live instead of a recorded voice.

Q. *Should I leave a personal message on a business answering machine?*

A. This depends on just how personal your message is. If it is a "welcome back" call after an illness or holiday, or a happy birthday or congratulations wish, then it is all right to leave the message, although it is preferable to call the home of an associate who is also a friend. Messages confirming or canceling social plans may also be left on business answering machines. Messages about aspects of your relationship, personal problems, or just plain gossip should never be left on any machine, but if it is the only way you can reach someone, you may leave a message that you would appreciate a return to your call, when convenient, after business hours.

Q. *We have a new facsimile machine (fax) in the office. It is changing the way we do business. What rules govern its use?*

A. The invention of the fax has made it possible for instant transmittal of data and indeed has changed the way that many companies do business. As with any other kind of office equipment, however, it can be abused. Rules governing the use of a fax are established in different companies. Some companies prefer that only certain employees be trained to use the fax or be allowed to use it, and naturally these rules should be followed. Additionally, faxes should never be used for personal communications. It may be a really fast way to send a birthday greeting to a friend in a branch office or at another company, but it is neither private (most faxes are placed in a central location in an office) nor inexpensive, and having fun with a fax can cost your company a lot of money and possibly cost you your job!

Q. *Are there any rules governing the use of electronic mail?*
A. The same common sense guidelines that apply to the use of the Fax and 800 numbers apply as well to using your computer, at company expense and on company time, to communicate with friends. Don't do it. Beyond that, electronic mail should be used for those memos and communications which require immediate answers or which respond to urgent requests and should be entered as professionally as a letter or memo would be written.

Q. *Should faxes be handwritten or typed?*
A. A facsimile machine should be considered a substitute for the mail. Therefore, a document transmitted by fax is no different than a document sent through the mail. A business letter would be typed; a quick note or sheet of figures might be handwritten; a draft of a report requested ahead of time by fax would probably be in rough form. Just because the communication means is instant does not mean the communication should be sloppy, any more than regular business correspondence sent through the post office would be sloppy. Unlike mailed communications, a fax-transmitted document requires a cover sheet specifying the number of pages being sent, including the cover sheet in the count, so that the recipient knows that he or she has received the entire document.

Q. *Is it acceptable to hand write business envelopes?*
A. Yes, it is acceptable as long as your handwriting is legible and neat. It is preferable, however, that they be typed, which is standard business practice.

Q. *What can I do when my supervisor listens in on my phone conversations?*
A. The answer to your question depends on why he is listening. If it is company policy that calls between the staff and customers are monitored by supervisors as part of a performance review of how employees deal with the public, then you should have been told this when you were hired or when the policy was established. If no such policy exists, then your first approach is to handle the fact that he is listening as an accident. When you know that he is listening, stop your conversation and say politely "I'm sorry, I'm on this line." Don't continue the conversation until the supervisor hangs up. If it happens more than once or twice, speak to your supervisor. Tell him that you have noticed that he is listening to your conversations and ask him if there is any business reason or policy behind his doing this or some problem that makes him feel he must monitor your calls. If there is no reason and your confronting him does not stop this behavior, then go to the personnel department. Make sure, however, that you are not spending valuable company time with long personal telephone calls and that your telephone time is legitimate before lodging a complaint.

Q. *It sometimes seems I spend my day playing "telephone tag," endlessly returning missed phone calls. Is there a way around this dilemma?*

A. Depending on the nature and length of the message or content of your call, efficient use of answering machines and office staff can alleviate some of this problem. If you are returning a call that was an information request and cannot reach the other party, leave the answer with the secretary or person answering the telephone. If you really need to discuss the information with the person you are calling, make a telephone appointment, leaving a message with the time you can be reached (and then be there) or the time that you will call back. If you have a request, leave your request on the answering machine or with the secretary, stating that you will call back at a specified time to see if there is an answer. It isn't always necessary to speak directly with the party you are calling when an assistant can obtain the information from him or her.

Q. *How can I politely terminate a telephone call with a business associate who talks endlessly?*

A. By telling him the truth—that you are very busy and have to hang up. Say, "Howard, that is a terrific story. I have one for you next time we talk, but I have got to go now—they're starting to line up outside my office, and I've got a report to finish. I'll get back to you tomorrow with the answer to your question about the quarterly statement. Talk to you then! Good-bye." If this is an on-going problem, you have to direct the content of the call by saying, "Howard! Great to hear from you. I have exactly three minutes before I'm due at a meeting, so we'd better get right to business."

Q. *Is there a way to handle a person who calls continually with important questions but is so disorganized that the call takes forever while she hems and haws through them? I don't like to be rude, but she takes an inordinate amount of my time on a regular basis.*

A. You could request that she use the facsimile machine to transmit her questions to you so you have a copy in hand when you talk on the telephone. This forces her to organize her thoughts and gives you the chance to address each question in an orderly fashion. If she doesn't take the hint and follow this procedure in the future, say politely, "Carol, I am on very limited time and feel we could get through these questions a lot faster if you had them organized before you call. Could you try writing them down, in order, before you call in the future?"

For Co-workers
and Supervisors

Q. *Should I visit my boss when he is in the hospital? What about co-workers?*
A. No, you should not. It is assumed that persons who are hospitalized are very ill or in pain, and the only visitors should be close friends and family members who do not require entertaining. It is highly unlikely that a boss or a co-worker wants to be seen at his or her worst by those in front of whom he or she would never otherwise wear pajamas or hospital gowns. Sending flowers, a book to read, magazines, cards and notes, however, are gestures that indicate you are thinking of the person and wishing him or her well.

Q. *Is it all right to call a supervisor or co-worker when they are in the hospital?*
A. As soon as you know the person is feeling well enough to receive calls, you may place a very brief call to extend your wishes for a fast recovery to full health, particularly if you have a close relationship. You should not gossip or present a litany of all the events which have occurred in the office since his or her hospitalization, unless he or she asks you to. And al-

though it sounds reassuring, you should not say words to the effect of, "We're doing fine here without you!" any more than you should say, "The place is falling apart without you." Either of these statements is guaranteed to cause stress for the hospitalized person. If asked, simply say, "Well, we're managing. But we all miss you, and everyone sends you best wishes." You also should not ask for a rundown on his or her surgery or illness. After extending a greeting, you may ask if there is any way you can help or anything you can do and then be the one to terminate the call.

Recovery is a fatiguing experience, which makes talking on the telephone tiring for the hospitalized person.

Q. *How do we treat a chronically ill employee?*
A. When you are aware that a co-worker has a serious illness, it is not your place, unless you have a close relationship, to pry into her condition. If she has told you of her condition, you naturally would ask, periodically, how she is feeling, but you mustn't dwell on it. As long as she is at work, it is expected that she will do her job as she did it before, and her health is not a cause for alarm or distress on your part, or for you to treat her any differently than you did before. This is true whether she has AIDS, epilepsy, diabetes, or cancer. No matter how you feel, she is trying to function as she did before, and you must allow her the dignity to do this. If there is a chance that she will have a setback or attack while at work, it is important that she inform her supervisor and any close co-workers so

that they know how to assist her, but this information is still no reason to treat her differently.

Q. *A co-worker has been hospitalized for a nervous breakdown and is coming back to work. How should I treat him?*
A. Welcome him back and carry on as usual. Do not ask what happened, what his treatment was like, or where he has been. Should he want to discuss his breakdown, he will. In this case, be responsive and listen, but do not bring it up as a topic of discussion again unless he does.

Q. *How can we help a staff member who isn't carrying his share of the work load because of his illness?*
A. Assuming that the company management is aware that he is unable to fulfill all the obligations of his job but is permitting him to continue at work out of consideration for his self-esteem and dignity, you can assist in subtle ways. You can take turns telling him you are caught up and offer to help him research or write a project or help him plow through an overflowing correspondence file. If his illness is temporary, you can each quietly offer to help him out now, and, to help him feel less indebted, that you know he'll return the help when he feels better. If, however, his work load is taking a considerable amount of your time, you have to weigh your desire to help against the fact that you are doing two jobs for one paycheck! In this case, you should make an appointment with your supervisor and review the situation.

If you are the supervisor and, as management,

have decided to work around the employee's inability to complete all his tasks, it is incumbent upon you to explain the situation to the staff and to solicit their help. Outline to them the available options, including paid overtime for the extra work they will have to do, the possibility of hiring a temporary staff member to help, or the rescheduling of deadlines or reassigning of responsibilities. You are the one who has to balance consideration for the ill employee with consideration for the well, without taking advantage of the latter.

Q. *One of my co-worker's husband died. Should I have gone to the wake or the funeral? I sent a sympathy card but wonder now if that was enough.*

A. The answer to your question depends on the closeness of your relationship with your co-worker. If you have been working together for quite a while, if you socialize outside the office, or if your work day brings you in frequent contact with one another, then it is appropriate to attend either the wake or the funeral service or both if you wish. In addition, you may send a note expressing your sympathy or flowers to the home of your co-worker. If you have only a nodding acquaintance with one another, then a card with a personal note inscribed is sufficient.

Q. *What is the role of an employer when there is a death in the family of an employee?*

A. If the person who has died is a spouse or child, then attendance at the wake or funeral is appropriate. In addition, many companies have a budget for flowers or contributions to a fund after a tragedy strikes an employee so that arrangements through the company may be made. If no budget exists, then funeral flowers or contributions from your department may be sent, either charged to your own contingency fund or with contributions from department members. A personal offering of flowers or a contribution to a charity is also appropriate. Most important is a telephone call offering sympathy and support, and help, if required. Such a sad occurrence transcends the most distant employer/employee business relationship and requires that an employer be supportive and express concern. If the person who has died is an aunt, parent, cousin, or more distant relative, a note of sympathy is all that is required.

Q. *I'm getting a divorce. It is a difficult time for me and it sometimes affects my work. What should I tell my supervisor and the people I work with?*
A. You should definitely tell your supervisor, privately, that you are going through divorce proceedings and that you are finding that it sometimes affects your work. She may have noticed that something is wrong, and it is important that she be told so she can make necessary allowances and not think that you are just taking your job lightly. It is not necessary to tell co-workers unless you want to or unless they are particularly close. If you do want to tell them, apologize for being distracted sometimes and thank them for their patience, without going into detail or taking office time to dwell on your problems with them.

Q. *I keep my private life separate from my professional life. I'm getting a divorce and need to take time off occasionally for meetings with my lawyer, but I don't want my co-workers to know. Should I invent fictitious doctor appointments to explain my absences?*

A. You do not need to explain your absences to your co-workers, only to your supervisor, with whom you have to work out how you will make up the time. Be sure you let your supervisor know that you are not telling anyone in the office and ask that she not tell anyone, either. If a co-worker asks where you are going, just smile and say you have an appointment out of the office. You might say you will be back in two hours, or won't be back that day so telephone messages can be relayed properly. If the co-worker is ill-mannered enough to persist in demanding to know where you are going, repeat that you have an appointment, and that your supervisor is aware of it and can certainly reach you in an emergency.

Q. *What should I do if I suspect a co-worker of theft?*
A. A suspicion is not enough to make a charge against someone, and you could cause irreparable damage to both the co-worker and yourself if you make an unsubstantiated allegation. This is very serious, and you need to be very careful and not jump to conclusions—there may be conditions of which you are unaware. If you are able, you should discuss your suspicions with the co-worker, giving him a chance to explain or to alleviate your concern. If, indeed, theft is involved and the situation will not be corrected by the co-

worker, then you should report your concern to your supervisor and let her handle it from that point on. Do not discuss it with other associates or co-workers, however. To do so would be to gossip and perhaps to put yourself in the position of being sued for slander if your suspicions turn out to be unfounded.

Q. *What should I do if the boss asks me to make coffee?*
A. If the request is a one-time favor before a meeting, for example, there is no reason to refuse. If the request is for daily coffee making and you object, try not to get huffy. Suggest that since you both drink coffee, whoever gets in first will start it brewing and that you take turns cleaning the pot, bringing in milk, buying the coffee, etc. so that it isn't a burden for either of you. If several people in the office drink the coffee, suggest a rotating schedule for everyone who does, including your boss, so you can take turns and share the chore. Even if you don't drink coffee, you can organize the schedule and post it by the coffee pot. If your boss absolutely insists that it is your job and it was not discussed when you were interviewed and hired, and if she refuses your suggestions to share the job, then you have a legitimate reason to go to the personnel department and complain.

Q. *I work in an office where collections are always being taken for this one's new baby or that one's marriage, and I resent it. What can I do about it?*
A. You can simply refuse, you can say you are planning to give your own gift or card (but be sure you really do), or you can suggest one set amount of

money to be collected from everyone, once a year, to go into a "pot," with the money to be allocated for wedding or baby gifts, funeral remembrances, or get-well gifts. You can also safely assume that most of the others feel as you do and suggest, at a staff meeting, that department gifts be eliminated in the future, leaving it to each person to acknowledge events on his or her own. If there is a consensus that this would be a relief and is a good idea, it becomes policy. If most people want to continue to send joint gifts, those who do can sign their names to the card and those who don't won't feel obligated to participate once the situation is brought into the open and discussed.

Q. *In my office someone is always bringing in a cake to celebrate a birthday or promotion or farewell. My birthday is coming up, and I'd prefer not to celebrate at work. How can I discourage any fuss being made?*
A. There is usually one person who is the office "organizer" for these celebrations. Speak to him or her and say that, although you appreciate the thought, your preference is to observe your birthday quietly at home and that you would be grateful if she would be sure no fuss is made. If, for some reason, you cannot do this, then tell your closest associate in the office what your feelings are and ask that he or she help you out and put a stop to any party plans in your honor.

Q. *My boss left a number where she can be reached on vacation. How do I know whether or not to call?*
A. If you are not sure of your own judgment, ask your boss, when she gives you the number, exactly

what she considers valid reasons for you to call. Ask her, too, what she expects to have come into the office during her absence and which of those things she needs to know about while she is away. Also ask her if she wants the number given to anyone else and if so, who.

Q. *My boss knows I'm vacationing at home this year. He's called me several times already, and I've been gone only two days. I'm not saying I'm indispensable, but how can I get him to leave me alone?*

A. This year there is not too much you can do, except for telling him, the next time he calls, that you plan to take several day trips and will be unavailable, so perhaps he had better think if there is anything else he might need while you are on vacation because you won't be able to get back to him during office hours.

Next year, anticipate this problem and be sure to leave an inventory of where things are located in your files or in the office. Review it with your boss before you leave. If there will be a temporary person covering your job, ask if he or she could start the day before you leave so you can familiarize him or her with the office. Leave the temp and your boss both a copy of your inventory, notes, or lists.

Q. *I am a smoker and am aware that fewer and fewer people smoke at work these days. Is it okay for me to smoke in my work space?*

A. The answer to your question is twofold. First, there are many local ordinances governing smoking in buildings, and there is often company policy against smoking. Check with personnel on both. If there is no ordinance and no policy, then the second part of the answer has to do with courtesy. Ask co-workers nearby if your smoking would bother them. If it would, then don't. If it wouldn't, it still is best not to smoke often in a shared space if you are the only one who smokes. If there are no prohibitions against it, you may smoke in your own, enclosed office.

Q. *Two of my co-workers don't get along very well. I have to work with both of them, sometimes together. How should I handle their petty squabbles?*
A. Since their behavior is inappropriate in the office, you can feel free to tell them so, and that you find it counterproductive and distracting, particularly when you are working together with both of them. You should be very businesslike and not attempt to mediate or get caught up in taking sides or reasoning with them. If they continue and you really find it impossible to work, then tell them you are going to have to speak to your supervisor if they don't stop immediately.

Q. *How do you tell a co-worker he has bad breath? Or body odor?*
A. The kindest way is to ask to speak to him privately, and then tell him. Say, "George, I think you are just terrific, so I'm taking a chance you won't be offended if I tell you that your breath can be really strong sometimes (or sometimes you have a strong body odor that is noticeable) and I would hate to have that stand in the way of the promotions you are sure to be considered for in the company. I'm really worried you

are offended that I've mentioned this, but I wouldn't feel like a friend if I didn't."

Q. *How do I respond when I'm asked what my salary is?*
A. With a smile and the statement "More than my boss thinks it should be, and less than I think it should be!" Then change the subject. Only the rudest person would insist on an answer. If so, you may reply in kind by saying "That is not an acceptable question and is nothing I care to discuss with you."

Q. *What can we do about a forgetful boss? Often he says "I'll check on that and get back to you." How long do we wait to remind him? What do we say?*
A. Unless you need the information urgently, wait two to three days and then remind him by saying, "You said you would let us know about [whatever], and we're at the point where we really need the information to go ahead. Is there any way we can help find the answer, or do you think you may have it today?"

Q. *My secretary is superb, and I would like to find some way to thank her for the extra work she has done, in addition to increasing her salary. Since we maintain strictly professional relationships in our company, with little personal socializing among ranks, I am concerned that it might be awkward to take her to lunch and that it might not be a really sufficient way to thank her. Can you offer any suggestions?*
A. One very nice way to say thank you is to acknowledge her life outside the office and give her two thea-

ter, ballet, or concert tickets, with an enclosed note expressing your appreciation for her extra effort and hopes that she and her husband (or a guest if she is unmarried) will enjoy the evening. If she has young children, enclose baby-sitting money! You could also give her a mental health day or two off (not to be entered in her personnel record) if she has been putting in an exceptional amount of time. Or arrange for a gift certificate for dinner at a nice restaurant for her and her family—especially nice thanks if additional work she has done for you has kept her overtime and away from her family. What is really important is that you tell her thank you and acknowledge her effort. Believe it or not, that means more than any other gift you could give!

Q. *My boss has sent flowers to my home on two occasions in thanks for extra work I have done for him. My husband takes exception to this and says it is not appropriate. Is it?*
A. It is not only appropriate but very thoughtful for your boss to thank you for your extra effort. The fact that he chooses to send flowers to your home rather than give them to you in the office does not mean that he is being too familiar or intruding on your home life but rather that he wants to thank you personally.

Q. *There is someone who works for me who is extremely bright but who has dreadful taste in clothing. This makes him ineligible for promotion, since the job he would be slated for is very public. How can I talk with him about this without seeming discriminatory or offensive?*

A. It's easy. Describe the job to him and tell him you'd like to offer it to him, but that corporate guidelines require a certain style in dressing. Explain that his style is fine for what he is doing now, but that he would have to modify it for the new job. Tell him that you realize this requires a substantial investment, and that, on a one-time-only basis, the company would like to offer him a wardrobe allowance to get started. Tell him, too, that he would be accompanied by a stylist for his selections. Hire a personal shopper or consultant to do just that. It's worth the investment of a few thousand dollars to put the right person in the job, and if you have the faith in him that you imply, the return on your investment will be there (and he will have the sense to consult the consultant for future additions to his wardrobe!).

Q. *The company messenger has begun calling me by my first name, which I don't mind but which is inappropriate in our very formal company. May I request that he stop, or would that seem imperious?*

A. No, it's not imperious if the company is that formal, but perhaps a gentler way to do it would be to say, privately, "Ben, I hope you'll continue to use my first name when we're alone, but company rules are that we use 'Mr.' [or Ms or Miss or Mrs.] when other people are around." He'll get the message.

Q. *When my boss's wife calls, she often asks me for details of what is happening in the office. What should I do?*

A. Be polite. Say something innocuous like, "It is incredibly busy—everyone has at least two projects too many, but we're managing!" and tell her you will connect her or offer to take a message. If she presses for specific answers that border on gossip, or you feel uncomfortable answering, just say, "Gee, I haven't any idea! You'll have to ask John (or Mr. Briggs, or however you address your boss). Let me tell him you are on the line."

Q. *My boss's husband often picks her up at night after work. He sometimes has to wait, and he spends the time talking to me, which means I don't get my work done. What should I do?*

A. When you are frantically busy, just say, "I would love to talk to you some more, but I have a deadline on this project in about one minute and have to get back to it!" And then get back to it, with a smile for him. If he doesn't take this hint and persists in chatting, offer him a magazine or a comfortable chair some distance from where you are working with an apology for being so busy. If he doesn't move, then you have no choice but to pick up your work and, again with a smile, tell him you hope to see him soon but that you must be on your way (to the copy machine, another floor, the ladies room, etc.) and then find a quiet corner to do your work until he leaves. Since he is the boss's husband, there will be times when it is just all in a day's work to entertain him until your boss is ready to leave. Sometimes, considerate etiquette requires setting aside what we would rather be doing or tolerating the inappropriate but well-intentioned behavior of others.

Q. *I run a small company that is part of a larger office building. My company uses the custodial services the building provides. Should I tip the custodians, the doorman, or the building manager at Christmas?*
A. Yes, you should, just as you would if you lived in an apartment building that provided those same services. Your monetary gift should be enclosed in a card with a greeting from you that wishes each of them a good holiday and a happy new year and should be signed by you with your company name below your name.

Q. *One of the benefits of employment with my company is paid membership in a private club. Do I tip employees, or do I assume the company or my boss takes care of that?*
A. No, you should not assume the company or your boss takes care of it, other than by a contribution at the holidays to the employee holiday fund. Individual service given you by club staff should be rewarded by you, personally, at holiday time. Additionally, any special services provided to you by club employees should be rewarded by tips throughout the year as services are rendered. You would tip a locker room attendant, a washroom attendant, or a headwaiter, for

example, but not a lifeguard, a nutritionist, or a secretary.

Q. *Should I give a holiday gift to my boss? He has always given me one in the past, along with others in the department, but I didn't think I was supposed to give one to him.*

A. It is not necessary that you reciprocate with a gift for him, unless you have a close working relationship and would like to express your appreciation for that relationship with a gift. Your gift should not be of a personal nature. It may, however, be something like a book about a topic you know he is interested in, a desk accessory for his office, or a food item or bottle of his favorite wine or aperitif.

Q. *Should I give a holiday gift to the people who work for me?*

A. It is customary that, in a small department, the supervisor gives gifts to his or her employees at the holidays. The gifts should be of equal value for persons of equal responsibility and should not be personal care items or clothing. In a large department or division, it is not customary or possible to give gifts to all employees, but it is very nice to extend holiday greetings and a handshake before the holidays and a personal wish for a happy and healthy new year. If you wish, holiday cards may be sent to the homes of your employees, as well.

Greetings and Meetings

Q. *Business greetings used to begin with a handshake. Now many seem to begin with a kiss. What is appropriate and what isn't?*

A. Kissing is a very personal way of saying hello, so you have to be careful about using it in business situations. Don't kiss someone you don't know well. They might recoil in surprise or embarrassment, which is awkward for both of you. Generally speaking, the longer you have known a person and the more established your social and business relationships, the more appropriate a friendly peck on the cheek is likely to be for both parties. Take into consideration the occasion and the setting. Kisses exchanged in the context of business meetings that are social in nature, such as banquets and conventions, may be acceptable. Those exchanged in pure business settings such as conference rooms or offices should be replaced with a handshake. Avoid kissing up or down the ranks. A junior person kissing a senior executive appears to be currying favor. The opposite can suggest that you're taking advantage of your higher position to make inappropriate advances toward a subordinate.

Q. *I'm not comfortable kissing someone hello when I know them only through business. How can I avoid being kissed?*

A. Don't ever feel obligated to give or to receive kisses. Keep your distance and extend your hand before the kisser has a chance to get too close. Good feeling can be extend with a smile and words such as "It's really great to see you," accompanied by a warm handshake.

Q. *A woman with whom I do business really caught me off guard with a hello kiss. I reacted very negatively. Do I owe her an apology?*

A. It would smooth things over if you immediately said "I didn't mean to offend you—you caught me off guard, but I really am very glad to see you!" if you are alone, or, if others are present, at a moment when you can speak to her privately. If she is astute, she will make a mental note that you do not regard a hello kiss favorably and will not repeat it in the future.

Q. *Who shakes hands with whom in business situations?*

A. Social hand-shaking codes are relaxed in business situations where it is assumed that people meeting for the first time or after not seeing one another for a while will shake hands as a natural part of their greeting, no matter what their rank in relationship to one another and no matter what their gender. When you are introduced to someone, either one of you may extend your hand first. Your handshake should be relaxed but firm (never limp), and you should look the other person in the eyes, smile, and say "I am very pleased to meet you" or give another cordial greeting. Do not hold on to the other person's hand or pump his or her arm. If someone you are meeting seems to back off, do not force a handshake. If he does not respond to your offer to shake hands, simply drop your hand back to your side, smile, and say "Hello."

Q. *I am not at all clear as to the proper way to introduce people to one another and always end up getting tongue-tied or even avoiding making an introduction. Can you give me the guidelines?*

A. The only difference between the rules for social introductions and the rules for business introductions is that women are not treated as women but are introduced according to their business rank. To begin with, each person is always introduced to the other. This can be achieved in two ways. First, by actual use of the word "to": "Mr. Johnson, I'd like to introduce you to Mrs. Borden." Second, (and most generally used), by saying the name of the person to whom the other is being introduced first, without using the preposition "to": "Mrs. Borden, may I introduce Mr. Johnson."

The three basic rules in social introductions are:

1. A man is always introduced to a woman.

2. A young person is always introduced to an older person.

3. A less important person is always introduced to a more important person. Socially this can be difficult, since it is sometimes hard to determine who is most important.

In business introductions, there is one basic rule: a less important person is introduced to a more important person, whether male or female. If the executive vice president, Allan Palmer, and the new product vice president, Jennifer Cato, have not met, you would introduce them by saying, "Allan, this is Jennifer Cato. Jennifer, Allan Palmer." When introducing the new office manager, Valerie Adams, to the company president, Loretta Polhill, you would say, "Mrs. Polhill, I would like you to meet Valerie Adams, our new office manager. Valerie, this is Mrs. Polhill, our company president." When introducing people of equal rank in business situations, social rules apply—a man is introduced to a woman, and a younger person to an older person.

Do not use first names in business introductions, unless it is the office custom, or with a business client or customer until requested to do so.

Q. *When introducing business associates to one another in social situations, should I mention what they do or something about them?*
A. Yes, because it helps those you are introducing to begin a conversation with one another without having to ask, "What do you do?" Say, "Burt, I'd like you to meet Philip Greer. Phil is the head of marketing at Andrews International and a real Rams fan, as well. Phil, this is Burt McQuade, our account executive at Myers and Myers. Burt is a Giants fan, but given their season this year, you might make a convert out of him." In this way, you give each person two topics of

instant conversation—their jobs and their shared interest in football. You may stay and join in their conversation or, if pressed to make other introductions, excuse yourself and move on.

Q. *Several United States senators will be touring our facility next month. How should they be addressed and introduced?*
A. They are addressed as "Senator" or "Senator Johnson" and are introduced as "Senator Johnson" or "Senator Johnson of Alabama." The form of the introduction would be to present company people to the senator: "Senator Johnson, I would like you to meet Jennifer Schmitt, our Vice President of Personnel. Jennifer, this is Senator Johnson of Alabama."

Q. *Should I stand when a co-worker enters my office?*
A. Only when it is the first time you are meeting. Since co-workers are in and out of one another's offices frequently throughout the day, it is unnecessary to leap to one's feet at every entry. See "Especially for Men" and "Especially for Women" for guidelines on when to stand for other visitors.

Q. *If a co-worker stops by your office to ask a question, do you invite her to be seated, rise to greet her, or remain seated while she stands in the doorway? What if the person who drops by is your boss?*
A. A quick question asked from the doorway does not require you to serve as host and seat your co-worker, which would probably extend the question into a visit, nor does it require that you stand to an-

swer the question. If the person is your boss, whether he or she enters your office or remains in the doorway, no matter whether you are a man or a woman, rise from your chair to speak with him. If he sits down, naturally you would then return to your desk and be seated as well.

Q. *How do I introduce my secretary to business associates or clients?*
A. Always by name, never just by title, as in "Henry, this is my secretary." If your secretary prefers to use her first name, you would say, "Henry, I would like you to meet my secretary, Susan Verlin. Susan, this is Mr. Livingston." If, on the other hand, Susan prefers to use her last name, you would substitute "Mrs. Verlin" for "Susan Verlin." It is up to Mr. Livingston to say "Please call me Henry" when meeting Susan.

Q. *When new clients whom my boss hasn't met arrive, how do I greet and then introduce them?*
A. It is appropriate for you to rise from your seat, say "Hello, I'm Cindy Young, Mr. Harris's secretary," shake hands, and then ask the client to be seated while you notify Mr. Harris that he has arrived. When your boss is ready to see Mr. Harris, you would again rise, ask Mr. Harris to accompany you, and upon escorting him into your boss's office, say "Mr. Greenfield, this is Mr. Harris." Their further greeting is up to them, and you may return to your own work.

Q. *When is it acceptable to close your office door?*
A. Whenever you are conducting a meeting confidential in nature, you would close your office door to

ensure that what is said remains confidential. It is also acceptable when you are doing work that requires close concentration to preclude a casual drop-in visit by a co-worker. Most people understand that a closed door indicates that you do not wish to be disturbed at the moment.

Q. *When should a closed-door meeting be interrupted?*
A. In the case of an emergency situation where an immediate response or answer is needed of someone behind the closed doors, one may interrupt a closed door meeting. If the message is confidential in nature, one would ask the person who the message is for to step to the door so it can be relayed quietly. It is also acceptable to write the nature of the situation or message on a piece of paper, knock on the door, wait to be admitted, and hand the paper to the person for whom it is intended. Never enter without knocking and waiting to be told to come in.

Q. *What are the rules for work spaces? Do you knock on the partition to get someone's attention or just walk in?*
A. You should either knock or say the person's name from the entrance to his work space out of respect for the fact that it is indeed his "space" before entering. You would treat entrance to a partitioned space just as you would entrance to a private office.

Q. *Once and for all, when entering or leaving an elevator do men stand aside and let women go first?*
A. I have seen elevator doors open and close before anyone has a chance to enter the elevator while every-

one is standing politely back to let someone else go first. Often, a man will enter the elevator first so that he can hold the door or the "open" button for others entering. A junior executive would do this for senior executives and visitors as well. However, scanning the crowd to see who is male or female or junior or senior can lead to missed elevators, and the general rule is that the person closest to the door enters first and holds the door for those following. Exiting the elevator is exactly the same—those directly in front of the door get off first, with no difference paid to rank or gender.

Q. *When you are the first to arrive for an in-house meeting, how do you know where to sit?*
A. If it is your first meeting, you don't. Either wait for the chairperson to arrive to indicate a seat for you or ask "Where would you like me to sit?"

Q. *Are there any guidelines about who sits where for an in-house meeting? What if the meeting includes staff and non-staff visitors?*
A. Yes, there are guidelines. If the seating is at a rectangular table, the chairperson sits at the end of the table farthest from the entrance to the room. The seats on either side of the chair are for senior management and guests of honor. The seat at the end of the table opposite the chair is best for someone making a presentation. An alternative seating plan, when a guest of equal rank from another company is in attendance, would be for the chairperson to sit at the center of the table, flanked by his or her senior officers, facing his

or her peer from the other company, with the visitor's senior officers to his or her right or left. If the conference table is round, the seats to the near right or left of the chairperson are left for senior executives.

Q. *Are there particular guidelines as to what to do during a business meeting?*
A. Meeting manners are very important, and really parallel social manners. Be on time. Introduce yourself to others, and when seated, sit upright. It is not good manners to doodle, play with pens or pencils, drum your fingers, yawn, or make any offensive noises. Do not interrupt, but do be prepared to speak when called upon or when there is a time in the meeting for questions or comments. This means that it is important to do your homework and before the meeting to outline information you want to request or to share. Keep your comments relevant to the discussion, and keep them concise. Do not smoke unless it is permitted, and then only if it will not bother those around you. Do not request refreshments, although certainly accept them if offered, if you wish, but be careful not to spill, slurp, or make other eating or drinking noises. When the meeting is over, clean up after yourself and thank the chairperson on the way out.

Q. *Are there meeting manners for someone chairing a meeting?*
A. The first sign of good meeting manners is to show consideration for others' schedules. If, for example, you expect the meeting to be a long one, don't call it

for late afternoon, causing everyone to have to extend his or her workday and leave late from the office. It is thoughtful to inform those invited of the meeting date well in advance, and to issue the agenda ahead of the meeting so attendees have a chance to prepare. In the agenda, indicate how long the meeting will be, and stick to it. Indicate where people should sit, and be sure to introduce those who do not know one another. Start the meeting on time, which shows respect for those who have arrived on time, and maintain control of the meeting with combined tact and strength to control those who monopolize the meeting or deviate from the agenda.

Q. *When I am chairing a meeting, how can I politely cut someone off who is dominating a discussion?*
A. Interrupt the person, saying "Jean, you are making some really good points, but I am going to have to call 'time' on you for the moment to give someone else a chance to comment. We'll get back to you if time permits." If someone has strayed from the agenda, again interrupt, saying "Laura, what you are saying is important, but it is going to have to be the topic of another meeting or we'll never get through the list of things we have left on the agenda. Why don't you see me after this meeting so we can schedule some time to talk about your ideas?"

The Social Side
of Business

Q. *I never talk about politics or religion at social functions. Are there any verboten subjects at business functions?*

A. The same general conversational rules regarding politics, religion, and controversial or dubious topics apply at business functions. Additionally, never indulge in office gossip or speculation, and don't run on and on about your children or grandchildren. Certainly reply to questions about your family, but don't make it a topic that you initiate.

Q. *I was just told I was ill mannered because I didn't thank an associate at another company for the Christmas gift she gave me. Her gift was a thank-you for the business I gave her. Do I really have to thank her for a thank-you?*

A. Yes. Even though corporate gifts generally are thank-yous to you, courtesy dictates that they be acknowledged. It is much too late to write a thank-you now, but the next time you speak to your associate, you should mention the gift: "Genevieve, I've been meaning to tell you how invaluable the attaché case you sent me has become—it goes almost everywhere

I do, and I'm now lost without it!" or "Genevieve, I never told you how much we enjoyed the champagne! In fact, we drank a special toast to you the last time we opened a bottle—thank you so much!" That should make amends for this year. Next year, write or call immediately.

Q. *The office Christmas party is coming up. Every year it's employees only, where some employees partake more of the Christmas cheer than others and do and say things they invariably regret the next day. I've been on both sides of that fence. What, if anything, should be said the next day? And who should say it?*
A. The person who has made a fool of him- or herself should apologize for any harm done or offense given to another by his or her inappropriate behavior. Beyond that, nothing need be said by either the one who regrets his or her own actions, or by co-workers who observed it. Rehashing unfortunate or embarrassing moments serves no purpose except to create more embarrassment.

Q. *Is it proper for a woman to ask her male boss to dance at an office party? What about a female boss asking her male employee to dance?*
A. Certainly, so long as it is one dance only and most people are dancing. It would not be proper for a woman to repeatedly dance with either her boss or her employee, or to initiate dancing if no one else is.

Q. *How should holiday cards sent to a co-worker's home be addressed? Just to the co-worker or to the co-worker and spouse?*

A. Cards sent to a co-worker's home should be addressed to both the co-worker and his or her spouse, even if you have never met the spouse.

Q. *Should holiday cards be sent home or to the office?*
A. In many cases, you may not know the home address of a business acquaintance but still want to send him or her a card. In this case, the card would be sent to him or her only, at the office. If you do know the home address, then your card may be sent home, but should include the spouse's name.

Q. *My wife and I recently found out she is pregnant. Is there a proper way to announce this at work?*
A. As happy as you may be, pregnancy is not usually something that is announced in a formal way. Naturally you would share your good news with close co-workers, who will no doubt spread the word. If you really want everyone to know and there is a company newsletter, you could tell the editor, who will publish the news.

Q. *When I found out I was pregnant, some co-workers congratulated me and others asked if it was planned. I was speechless. How should I have responded to such an obviously personal question?*
A. I have found that a very effective way to respond to personal, prying, and ill-mannered questions is to look astonished and say "*What* did you say? I can't believe you meant to ask that question!" and then change the subject. In this case you could add, "I thought you could tell how really happy I am about

this great news!'' This does not dignify their rudeness with an answer, and it will make you feel better.

Q. *Is there a polite way to refuse a drink at a business lunch?*
A. No one has to drink, ever. When drink orders are taken, simply order a bottled water or a seltzer. There is no need to say "Oh, no! I never drink at lunch" or "I don't drink alcohol," which may make associates who have ordered a drink uncomfortable or defensive. Your ordering something to drink is more companionable than ordering nothing at all would be, enabling you to socialize with your associate or group without feeling as though you have to order an alcoholic beverage or make a personal statement by not ordering.

Q. *My boss is great. Is it acceptable to invite him to lunch for a special occasion like his birthday?*
A. No, it isn't. You may invite a peer or someone who works for you to lunch, but you may not invite your boss. Even if he occasionally invites you to lunch, this is one situation where the invitation is not reciprocated.

Q. *My co-workers and I have been invited to the boss's home for a dinner party. Should we bring the usual hostess gift?*
A. Yes. It would be more customary for each of you to select and take your own gift, but if the dinner party is just for you and your co-workers, you may all contribute to one gift from all of you.

Q. *After having had dinner at the boss's house, do we send a thank-you note to the boss and his wife at their home or at the office?*

A. Since the evening took place at their home and since they both entertained you, you would write them at home. To send your thank-you note to the office would look as though you were thanking only your boss and would slight his wife.

Q. *My husband and I have been invited to spend the weekend at my boss's country house. We do know there is household help, but we don't know what to expect, whether it will be formal or informal, or how we should treat the servants.*

A. As to how formal your attire needs to be, you have to ask. Ask your boss or, when responding to the invitation, ask your hostess. Simply say "We are so looking forward to the weekend—could you tell me if we need any special wardrobe items?" He or she will let you know if they dress for dinner, whether you need a swimming suit, tennis clothes, or just jeans and sweaters. Servants are greeted with a smile and hello, but not a handshake, and they are treated with courtesy. Don't make special demands of them, but do feel comfortable asking if you need a particular item— whether thread and a needle or an aspirin. Gratuities are given to a servant who presses your clothes or makes up your bed, but not at the time of the service. When you are ready to leave, give the maid or valet who has assisted you two or three dollars after a one-night visit and five dollars or more after a weekend.

If you do not see him or her, put the money in an unsealed envelope bearing his or her name and ask your host to deliver it for you. It is nice to include a note expressing your thanks. If there is a cook, butler, or chauffer, you do not tip them unless they have provided a service specifically for you. Opening the door, preparing dinner, refilling your wine glass, or driving you and your hosts somewhere are not considered personal services.

Q. *My wife and I have been invited for a weekend on an important client's yacht. Do we tip the crew? Is it okay to talk business during the weekend?*
A. As you would leave a tip for the maid who takes care of your room in a private home, you would leave a tip for the cabin steward who provides personal services on a yacht. You would thank the captain, upon your departure, for a pleasant trip, but not tip him, nor would you tip the dining-room steward, any more than you would tip the person who serves you at a dinner party in someone's home. It is certainly all right to talk business, since it is business which has brought you together, but not to the exclusion of the other members of the party, such as your wife, who are not involved in the business part of the relationship.

Q. *My co-workers and I often lunch together near the office. I don't drink, but they often do. How do we split the check?*
A. It is easiest to ask for separate checks when you first order. If this is not possible, then divide the food

portion of the bill equally and have those who ordered drinks split or take care of their own bar bill.

Q. *Our suburban office has a lovely cafeteria. When I'm working with clients for the day, we eat lunch at the cafeteria. Normally I'd sit with my co-workers. Should they join me and my guest?*

A. Not unless you feel your guest would enjoy their company and provide a social break in your workday. If you feel it would be awkward to sit alone with your guest with no explanation or hurt your co-workers' feelings, you can introduce your guest to your co-workers and then say "Joe and I have more business to go over during lunch, so we're going to find a quiet corner and not bore you with our discussion."

Q. *Who decides where to hold a business lunch?*

A. The person who does the inviting selects the restaurant, but he or she may certainly ask if the guest has somewhere he would like to go and should ask whether the guest has any dietary restrictions, particularly if he is from a culture where dietary prohibitions are a way of life.

Q. *Who pays for a business lunch? Is it acceptable to pay with cash?*

A. The person who issues the invitation pays. It is acceptable to pay with cash, although using a credit card is more discreet than piling money on the table in a restaurant and it ensures a receipt, required for expense account reimbursement. If meeting for lunch is something that happens in response to a statement like "We should get together for lunch next week" and is not a formal invitation issued by one person, then each person usually pays for his own meal.

Q. *I'm a businesswoman who hosts a fair number of business lunches. Sometimes I have a problem getting the waiter to give the check to me. How do I ensure that I receive the check?*
A. This really shouldn't be a problem if you have made a reservation in your name, since the maître d' and the waiter will know you are the hostess. If they don't seem to recognize the fact, however, you can make other arrangements for payment. You may remind the maître d' when you enter that the bill is to be given to you, or you may give your credit card to him ahead of time and on your way out add a tip and your signature. You can also do your business entertaining at a restaurant where you have established credit so that the restaurant will bill you at your office with your having no more to do than add tips, sign, and leave.

Q. *Are there any differences between a business lunch and a business breakfast?*
A. Only the time of day and the choice of places to meet. A business breakfast has certain advantages in that it can be briefer, does not include the option for cocktails, and does not interrupt the business day in the way that a lengthy business lunch can. The disadvantage can be that it is usually held on your own time, before regular business hours begin. Another option is to hold a business meeting outside the office at tea

time, around half past three or four o'clock. A business tea has the advantage of allowing you consecutive, constructive hours in the office (without the interruption of a midday, extended lunch), and a usually quiet environment for conducting your business.

Q. *When I am taking a client out to lunch or dinner, who leads the way into the dining room? What if the dinner includes spouses? Who sits where?*
A. If the client is a woman, she would follow the headwaiter into the dining room, and he would hold her chair and seat her. If the client is a man, either one of you may enter first, although it is courteous for you to indicate that he is to precede you. When the dinner party is a larger group or includes spouses, it makes more sense for the host to precede his guests into the dining room so he can indicate where they are to sit. If they precede him, they have to stand around the table until he enters and directs them. If you are a man and your wife is with you, she would act as hostess for you, lead the way (usually with the most important woman in the group), and seat guests.

If just two of you are dining, your guest is given the preferential seat, usually the one that faces the room or the view or is out of the stream of traffic. If you are hosting a group, the waiter or the host or both first seat women guests, with the seat at the host's or hostess's right for the guest of honor, and men and women alternating around the table.

If the seating is at banquettes, two people dining are usually seated side by side on the banquette with the table in front of them. In a smaller restaurant, the woman or male guest is seated at the banquette and the man or host on a chair opposite.

In a restaurant with booths, women enter first and sit against the far wall facing each other across the table, and the men sit next to them on the outside.

Q. *How long should a business lunch last?*
A. The lunch itself should last no longer than one and $1/2$ hours. If you are meeting an associate at a restaurant, you have to allow for travel time which, depending on the area, can be as long as the lunch. Accordingly, try to choose a location that is convenient for everyone attending.

Q. *My boss has told me I should entertain clients more often at lunch. In addition to selecting a convenient location, are there other guidelines for selecting a restaurant?*
A. Yes, there are. The key guideline is that you should never choose a restaurant where you haven't eaten before. You want to be sure that the service is prompt and unobtrusive and that there is a menu with a variety of selections.

Q. *Who should arrive first at a business lunch?*
A. The host should arrive first, preferably ten to fifteen minutes early to be sure the reservation is in order and to make certain the table location is one that permits uninterrupted business discussion and that is not in the mainstream of traffic. In addition, by being

there first, the host makes his or her guests feel welcome.

Q. *Is it proper to take notes during a business lunch?*
A. It is not improper, but it can be awkward. It is difficult to eat, focus on your associate, and manage a note pad and pen at the same time. Naturally should a topic arise on which you want to jot a reminder to yourself, you will want to have a pocket or purse notebook handy, but it should not be left on the table. If the purpose of the lunch is to review documents of any sort it would be best to do this after coffee has been served.

Q. *Sometimes I would prefer to entertain guests at luncheon in my office instead of in a restaurant. Is it all right to do this?*
A. This can be a wonderful way to entertain if your office and staffing lend themselves to your holding a lunch as a business person, not as a waiter and bus boy. It is important that you have someone to help you serve and clear the meal so you can concentrate on the business at hand. It is equally important, however, that you do not suddenly decide to invest in china, crystal, and table linens and expect your secretary to set the table, order the lunch, and then wash up afterward. Only if this has been discussed as a duty with your secretary, and he or she has agreed to it, or there are other personnel whose job descriptions would include kitchen time, should you even think of holding in-house lunches. Of course if you use the services of a

caterer, then all these elements would be taken care of.

Q. *I travel frequently on business and am the client of several corporations. Often, they suggest that we go out in the evening and have taken me to the theater and to concerts. Am I expected to pay for my ticket?*

A. No, you are not. You are their guest and can assume that any business entertainment with their corporate personnel will be paid for by them. If you are traveling to an area and have asked your host to obtain tickets for you to any event, you would pay for the tickets immediately and not expect them to pick up your personal entertainment costs.

Q. *Are there any rules for entertaining business associates and clients at home?*

A. There are no rules, but there are some guidelines which help make your gatherings successful. First, don't invite guests who do not have a logical connection to one another. If there is no connection, conversation will be difficult and/or the purpose of the entertainment becomes more social than business in orientation. Second, plan in advance so that you are not doing everything yourself. Get help from caterers or food suppliers. The point of business entertaining is not to have you so busy serving as working host that you never have time to talk to your guests. Third, don't entertain so lavishly that the perception your clients have of you is distorted or harmed. Keep everything relatively simple so that you have time to accomplish business while getting to know one another a little better at the same time.

Q. *How do I go about getting help for business entertainment? What qualifications do I look for?*

A. Whether you are entertaining for business at home or in the office, it is important that you find good, competent, and reliable help. There are several resources for this, beginning with word of mouth. Ask associates if they have recommendations. When you are at an event, it is perfectly appropriate to ask for a business card from a caterer who, in your estimation, is doing an excellent job. Many towns and cities have agencies which specialize in party help. Call them for rates and information—some require a minimum number of hours which may exceed your needs. Bartenders and waiters often have local chapters of their unions, which are listed in the yellow pages. The union office can make referrals. Local high schools and colleges may have employment services. To begin, call the information or main number and ask. If you receive no affirmative response, call the guidance office in a high school and the dean of student's office in a college. Local restaurants may, for a fee beyond the cost of the food and labor, be willing to provide food and service. Speak to the restaurant manager. Always check references.

When interviewing candidates, be clear on your expectations. Meet or speak in advance and discuss exactly what needs to be done, confirm the fee, and check whether gratuities are included in the bill.

Q. *I was recently invited to a business-related party by the host's secretary. Shouldn't he have called himself?*

A. Yes, it would have been more personal had he

called himself or sent a written invitation. His secretary can then handle any follow-through information, such as confirming the date and time with you or arranging additional details.

Q. *My wife and I frequently entertain for business, and try to remember personal information (likes and dislikes) about our clients, but it gets confusing with so many people to remember. Do you have any tips?*
A. Although this seems too systematic for some people, I have found it helpful to write down such things as client information, the date of the event, the place, and the special interests of the client and his or her spouse. You might include what you wore (to avoid a repeat performance) and personal information, such as the names of their children or hobbies or talents. Keep the information on file cards or in a filing system notebook and refer to it before the next time you see that client. He or she will appreciate your thoughtfulness and feel important to you. This, in turn, enhances your business relationship and future endeavors.

Q. *My husband and I own our own business, and clients often give us presents at holiday time. We send thank-you notes, but are we also expected to reciprocate with gifts?*
A. No, you are not. They are thanking you for the business you give them. Your thank you to them, in addition to your note, is (they hope), continued business.

The Retail Seller

Q. *At the supermarket it seems the cashiers are carrying on a conversation the entire time they're checking out my order. They don't seem to be paying attention to what they are doing. May I say something to the cashier, or should I speak to the store manager?*

A. You should speak to the cashier. Say "Excuse me, but I would appreciate it if you would pay attention to my order and continue your conversation later." If the cashier is rude to you or if your bill is not correct, then you should speak to the manager, or if you find the cashiers' chatting to be a constant problem, you should let the manager know how you feel privately, after your order is completed and packed up. There is no need to call him over or make a public scene in front of the cashier and other customers, which would be embarrassing to all of you.

Q. *At the store where I work, I often see parents who allow little children to run in and out of the clothes racks. Clothing is not inexpensive these days, and some of these garments are knocked to the floor and get dirty, but the parents don't even stop to pick up the clothing. Should I say something to the parent or the child?*

A. This depends on your store policy on dealing with customers. The next time this happens, inform the department manager and ask him or her how the situation should be handled. Generally, he or she would be responsible for asking the parent to control her child or to leave the department, or he or she would be the one to call store security if the situation continues. If the department manager tells you to handle it, then you would speak to the parent, not the child, saying "Excuse me, ma'am, but I have to ask you to keep your child with you—he is damaging the merchandise and I would hate for you to have to pay for all the clothing he has damaged."

Q. *Customers are always ready to ask for a supervisor if they don't like the service they get, but what can a salesperson do when faced with an obnoxious customer?*
A. Not a whole lot, unless store policy gives you carte blanche to be rude in return. The best thing to do would be to say "I'm very sorry that I don't seem to be able to assist you to your satisfaction. Let me get my supervisor and perhaps she can help you." Store management is aware that there are difficult customers, and they are trained to deal with them and are given the authority to handle these situations in specific ways.

Q. *When I'm shopping and just want to browse, how do I get rid of unwanted sales attention?*
A. Politely say "I appreciate your time and attention, but I am not ready to make a decision yet and really

need to look around some more. Tell me your name and I will ask for you if I decide to make a purchase."

Q. *Many times I've walked through a department store and been virtually showered with a spray of unwanted perfumes. It makes me angry. I pay good money for the perfume of my choice, and don't appreciate mixing scents. How can I stop this from happening?*
A. When you see a salesperson approaching with perfume samples, look her in the eye and say "No, thank you." It would be most unusual for her to persist in chasing you through the store in an attempt to spray the sample on you, and your no should deter even the most aggressive sprayer.

Q. *I work at a counter near the main entrance. Customers seem to think of my counter as an information desk, which I don't mind when I am not helping another customer. What do I say to someone who barges to the head of the line?*
A. If the person is trying to ask you a series of questions, say "I will be with you as soon as I am finished with this customer, who was here before you." If there is indeed a line of customers behind the one you are serving, you may say "I'm sorry, but there is a line of people ahead of you, and I'll have to ask you to wait your turn." If the person pushes to the front to ask where the china department is, it would probably save time and customer aggravation if you just tell her.

Q. *In the restaurant where I wait tables we are assigned specific stations with a certain number of tables.*

The hostess tries to seat customers equally between sta-
tions, but many times this just doesn't work out. Be-
cause tips are a large part of our income, we're not
allowed to work each other's stations. How do I respond
to a customer who asks me to take his order when the
waiter in that station is busy?

A. Since you don't pool your tips and since there
seems to be a rule about working each other's stations,
the best you can do is to say "I will tell your waitress
you are ready to order." If the customer appears agi-
tated, then speak to the hostess, who will have to fill
in until his waitress can get to him.

Q. *Skilled tradespeople are hard to find, I admit, but*
what can be done about the plumber who promises to
arrive at 9 a.m. and shows up at 5 p.m., or the delivery
that was guaranteed for noon but arrives in the middle
of dinner?

A. Actually, not a whole lot. You can express your
displeasure, but it probably won't make much difference. Many tradespeople work independently and do
not have a staff to call ahead and alert customers that
they will be late. Most do the best they can, but get
caught in emergency situations or in jobs that take
longer than they thought they would. If you have
complained and are not satisfied with the response,
then you have to take your business elsewhere.

Q. *I employ a cleaning woman once a week to clean*
my home while I'm at work. She has young children.
During school vacations she has asked me to allow her
to bring her children with her because no child care is
available. While I want to help this woman continue

to earn a living, I don't see how she can do her job well and keep an eye on her children, but if I don't agree I'll lose her services when school is back in session. What do I say in a situation like this?

A. You have every right to say no, explaining your feelings and suggesting that she look further for child care. If she can't or is unwilling to find a place for her children while she works, then you have to say you would like her to continue working for you when school resumes, so that she knows you will hold her job for her.

Q. *I work at a fast-food restaurant where people line up at a cash register and place their orders. Depending upon what people order, some lines move faster than others—through no fault or to no credit of those of us behind the counter. How do we respond when a customer makes a fuss?*

A. With a sincere apology and an explanation that you are all working as fast as you can. A smile and an expression of understanding can mollify most customers temporarily. If this is a persistent problem, the manager should be told, if he or she hasn't already noticed, that there is a lot of customer dissatisfaction so he or she can consider alternative means of moving people through the lines faster.

Q. *When something is knocked off a shelf in a store, who should pick it up?*

A. The person who knocked it off should, of course, pick it up. If he doesn't, then any employee who sees an item on the floor should pick it up and replace it.

Q. *I have found it more and more difficult to get help in department stores. If I am fortunate enough to find a salesperson, he has no idea where anything is and can't help me anyway. Is there any way to deal with this?*

A. The most effective way is to take your business elsewhere. With the large number of department stores which have gone out of business in the past few years, it is apparent that other people have felt as you do and have done just that. If, however, your shopping choices are limited and you need to continue to patronize these stores, then first try requesting the department manager. Explain your request, that you have not been helped to your satisfaction, and ask him or her for assistance with your purchase. If no department manager is to be found, then find the administrative offices and register your complaint. Unless someone was specifically rude to you, your concern has to do with the lack of informed help, and you needn't single out particular personnel.

Q. *I recently had lunch with a friend at a hotel. When I went to the ladies room, a woman in a uniform handed me one paper towel and then expected a tip. Was I supposed to give her money?*

A. It is customary to leave anywhere from 25 cents to one dollar for a bathroom attendant. The tip is for keeping the bathroom spotless and for rendering assistance—a safety pin for a fallen hem, a cold cloth were you feeling ill, a tissue to blot your lipstick, etc. Although you did not require assistance and were perfectly capable of obtaining your own paper towel to dry your hands, this is the way she earns her income, and it is expected that you leave something for her, her presence, and her efforts.

Q. *We used a babysitter hired through a babysitting service. She arrived inebriated and I sent her home. Should I complain to the service?*
A. Absolutely. She is a representative of that agency, and they need to know exactly how they are being represented. You needn't phrase your complaint nicely—after all, you had to cancel your plans, and they did not fulfill their part of your contract with them.

Q. *I am a restaurant manager. It is a family restaurant and is fairly casual. Some of the waitresses arrive for work with dirty fingernails or dirty uniforms or with hair that is sticking out in all directions. I know that is the style right now, but it looks almost unsanitary. It is hard to find good waitresses, and they are good at their jobs. How can I say something to them without losing them?*
A. You are the employer and are entitled to have standards. If you don't already have a written list of expectations, write one, including rules for personal hygiene. Their slovenly appearance reflects badly on your restaurant no matter how good the food or service. Give each waitress a copy of the list and explain that, should they not arrive for work clean and neat, they will be put on warning. Develop guidelines for hair—long hair is to be worn in a twist or bun, short

hair is to be brushed and neat. If they express an objection, explain that hair and food have never been an attractive team. They might have to forgo personal style to keep their jobs; but if you don't take these steps, you will lose your customers, and they will lose their jobs anyway.

Q. *Is there a polite way to deal with customers who eat a banana or an apple as they shop in my grocery store before it has been weighed at the check out? When enough people do this, it represents a loss to the store.*
A. There is really nothing you can do that won't put them on the defensive, since they most likely know they are wrong. You can say, "I'm sorry, but that hasn't been weighed yet. Would you please refrain from eating it until you have checked out?" They will not be pleased and may get huffy, but it is likely that they won't do it again. Your only alternative is to follow them to the register with another banana or apple and instruct the check-out person to weigh it with the other fruit and then return it to you, which is publicly embarrassing and will guarantee that the customer will shop elsewhere in the future.

Q. *What do I do about people who litter in my store? I have no desire to pick up their used tissues or gum wrappers and resent that they can't be bothered to find a waste receptacle.*
A. Say, rather loudly, "Excuse me. You just dropped something—I wouldn't want you to lose it." Then turn away and be busy doing something else instead

of standing, arms folded, staring at them. That is far more polite than shouting, "Don't litter my store."

Q. *How do I handle customers who try to return merchandise that never came from my store in the first place without offending them?*
A. You should have a clearly posted sign explaining your return policy—that merchandise must be accompanied by a receipt. Then be polite but firm in saying, "I'm very sorry, but we have never stocked that item—the person who gave it to you must have mistakenly misinformed you about where it was purchased." If the customer persists, direct him to your sign and explain that there are no exceptions to the policy. If you choose to soften your words, you could offer him the names of other stores that might sell that item and suggest that he check with the donor of the gift to see which of them it may have been.

Q. *Do you have any general advice for people who work in service jobs? I have worked in a variety of stores and restaurants and am frequently amazed at the attitude of my fellow employees.*
A. The key advice is that service personnel are not representing themselves; they are representing the establishment for which they work. Customers don't really care if a waitress has tired feet or a salesperson is in a bad mood because he had a fight with his wife. What they see is an extension of the store or restaurant. What they take away with them is often an impression made by that one person. If it is an unfavorable impression, they do not then think favorably of

the establishment. Service people who deal with the public are really ambassadors of the store or restaurant and have an obligation to leave their personal lives or problems at the door when they enter. No matter how tired a waitress's feet, she has been hired to do a job that extends beyond serving food. She, along with the quality of the food and the decor, *is* that restaurant to the customer. A sales person who is distracted, grumpy, or terse leaves the customer with a negative feeling about the store. He is being paid not only to ring up sales at the register but to do it graciously and in the image the store wishes to portray.

It is not, however, up to you to do anything about it. Management eventually notices an employee who is harming the image of the store or restaurant. Although a negative impression reflects on you, too, you cannot, as a peer, either be critical or put yourself in a position of offering suggestions or advice.

Everyday Office Etiquette

Q. *Is there a polite way to handle copy machine hogs?*
A. That's rather a strong term for someone who is copying a big job. He or she is not intentionally "hogging" the copy machine, but presumably performing a lengthy required task. If you have a real emergency, you have to say so and ask if you can interrupt. If your projects are of equal urgency, the problem has to go back to both of your bosses as to whose assignment takes priority (keeping the machine going while you ask). If your job is not particularly urgent and it is just a convenient time for you to make your copies, ask when the other person expects to be done and return. Someday, you will be the one with the lengthy copying assignment and surely you won't think of yourself as a "hog."

Q. *What does one do about people who are constantly interrupting a copying job to make "just one" copy?*
A. One of two things. Either let them "play through" or tell them you are awfully sorry but you are on a priority assignment and tell them the time you expect to be finished. Usually there are many people who have "just one" copy to make, and by

the time you have let each of them interrupt you, you could have finished your own copying. If your office is small, it is courteous to announce that you will be tying up the copying machine for a big assignment and that anyone who has copying might want to do it before you begin.

Q. *How do you handle rumors in the workplace?*
A. You stay as far away from them as you possibly can. If a rumor is shared with you, don't even make a comment, and certainly never repeat it. As with any other form of gossip, what you say could be repeated, and the rumor could even be attributed to you as it makes its way around the office. If you are a supervisor and get wind of a rumor that is detrimental to a person or to the company, you should make it clear that speculative talk is just that, speculative, and that anyone who has a question should bring it to you.

Q. *Is it acceptable to brush one's teeth in the office washroom?*
A. Yes, but only if you thoroughly clean the sink when you are finished. It is revolting to others to go to the sink to wash their hands only to find your spit-out toothpaste and food particles.

Q. *What should you do if you begin a coughing or sneezing fit in the middle of a meeting? In the middle of a business meal?*
A. Immediately cover your mouth, excuse yourself, and leave the meeting or the table. Return only when the fit is over and you are composed.

Q. *What is the etiquette of eating at your desk?*
A. Eat at your desk only at lunchtime. Don't spend your lunch hour running errands and then eat during company time, even if you can work and chew simultaneously. Simple rules of neatness should be followed. Leave no dirty cups or plates around. Wipe up crumbs or spilled liquids and be sure to throw away leftovers and disposable items in a trash container that is away from your and others' desks and that has a cover. The sight and odors of discarded food are unpleasant. Watching someone else eat falls short of pleasurable entertainment, so if you must eat at your desk, pay strict attention to your eating manners. Do not answer the telephone with your mouth full.

Q. *If a co-worker is eating at his desk, should he be expected to continue to do his job during that time?*
A. No, not if it is his lunch hour. The problem with eating at one's desk is that others assume one is available for work-related discussion or questions. If you are eating at your desk and are interrupted by co-workers on business matters, it is acceptable to say "I'm on my lunch hour right now, but as soon as I'm finished I will get back to you with an answer."

Q. *I am in the process of selecting personalized linens, glassware, china, and silver for our corporate dining room. Can you offer any suggestions as to how these items should be monogrammed?*
A. They can be marked with the initials of the company or with the company logo, if it is usable in this way. Think of size first. The monogram should be in

proportion to the size of the piece. Also think of the overall appearance—do you really want every single piece of table service to bear the monogram?

The cloths for long tables are marked on either side of the center, halfway between the table center and the edge. Small tablecloths, for square tables, should be marked at one corner, midway between the table center and the point. If the monogram is irregular, it would look best at a corner, while a squared monogram looks best set in line with the table edge. If you will be ordering luncheon napkins, not large dinner napkins, the monogram should be placed at the corner, usually at an angle; but depending on the design, it may be placed straight. To test how it will look, fold a napkin as it will be used on the table and draw in your monogram.

China may be marked at the edge or in the center, depending on the attractiveness of the design and other design elements on the china.

Glassware is usually etched at the center of the bowl of stemware and approximately at the center of tumblers. You may find that using just the company initials on glassware gives the most elegant appearance.

Monogrammed silver generally looks best when its inherent design is simple, with a simple style of initialing.

Q. *Part of my new job is to hire caterers and arrange corporate luncheons. What is the best way to work with a caterer?*
A. Before meeting with the caterer, have your facts

ready. Know the location and size of the room, the number of people you expect, the time frame, your budget, what supplies you have on hand (tablecloths, flatware, etc.), and what you need. Preferably, hold your meeting at the location where the luncheon will be served so that the caterer can get an idea of such things as proximity to a kitchen or workroom, available electrical outlets, etc. You also should have an idea of whether you want a buffet meal or one that is served, which makes a difference in amount of personnel the caterer needs to provide. Make a checklist for talking with the caterer. Include the following questions:

- Who will provide the tables, linens, crystal, china, and flatware?
- Who will provide the centerpiece and/or other floral arrangements?
- What will be the ratio of catering staff to the expected number of guests?
- If cocktails are served, will orders be taken and filled or will guests go to the bartender?
- If it is a buffet, will the staff man the buffet line or will guests help themselves?
- If it is a seated meal, what is the method of clearing the tables between courses (you don't want dishes and silver thrown clanking into metal bins or plates scraped and stacked in the vicinity of the guests)?
- If wine is served, will the staff see to pouring it or will bottles be on the tables?
- Will coffee and tea cups be refilled?

- If there is a speaker, what is the timing and the arrangement so staff is not clearing or making noise during the presentation?
- What will the serving staff wear?
- Will gratuities be included in the bill or do they need to be paid separately?
- If the building requires security clearance for anyone entering, how soon will you need personnel information on the catering staff in order to clear them and to provide passes?

If the caterer does not provide tables, linens, flowers, etc., ask if he has recommendations for vendors who do. If he provides linens, discuss color choices.

Once you have discussed the particulars and received an estimate, shake hands and tell the caterer you will be in touch with him shortly. If he is extremely busy, book the date tentatively, but sign nothing until you've had a chance to interview at least one other caterer.

When your party is in progress, keep watch. If something is wrong, it is your responsibility to alert the caterer to the problem. Don't be intimidated, even by the haughtiest of caterers—just remember that you (the one who made the arrangements) will get the blame if the soup is cold or the glasses spotty, and you have the right to request the excellent quality and service you are paying for.

Q. *If a businessperson arrives extremely early for a meeting, is it all right to keep him waiting until the appointed time?*

A. If your schedule is filled until the time of his appointment, you need not feel guilty about asking him to wait. If you are free when he arrives, however, it would be courteous to invite him in. It would free your schedule later and might even make points with your visitor to have you accommodate his early arrival.

Q. *With so many parents of school-age children working full time, it seems my staff members spend half the afternoon talking to their children on the phone—for everything from refereeing sibling rivalries to giving instructions on starting to cook dinner. I'm a parent myself and understand their concern, but I have a business to run. Have you any suggestions on how to handle the situation?*

A. Your understanding and empathy is admirable, but your problem won't go away by itself. You have to speak personally to those who are using company time for personal business and tell them it has to come to a screeching halt. It is up to them to work out alternative ways of dealing with problems at home. It is up to you to put a stop to it, and the best way to do that is to explain that, although they are physically at their desks, their attention is elsewhere and that this is unacceptable to the company.

Q. *I work for a small family-run business. The owner's children and grandchildren always seem to be running in and out of the place—and that makes it hard for me to get my job done. I'm concerned about saying anything to my boss because these are his rela-*

tives I'm complaining about. How do I make such a sensitive complaint?

A. You don't. Family-run businesses can be a joy to be a part of, but when you aren't part of the family, nothing you say against a member of the family will be well received. I'm afraid this is a case where you have to overlook the distraction or look elsewhere for a job.

Q. *What are the guidelines on business favors?*
A. Business favors occur on many levels and they must be asked and given with great care. Asking your secretary to pick up your laundry or your watch from the jeweler on her lunch hour is an inappropriate favor to ask unless you reciprocate and do the same for her on yours. This kind of request to any subordinate is really a forced favor. Nine times out of ten they will do it for fear of placing their job in jeopardy if they don't. The fact that someone works for you and is employed at your discretion does not imply an obligation on the employee's part to extend the job description to personal favors. Accordingly, they should be avoided.

Also keep in mind that favors, in general, are stored away in the favor-doer's mind for a future time when he needs you to reciprocate. Favors, therefore, should be kept within reasonable limits. They should not pose a hazard, require a tremendous investment of time or effort, or violate the ethics of either party. Asking for access to confidential records is an unreasonable, off-limits favor to request.

If you must ask a favor, phrase it in such a way that it is not uncomfortable for someone to refuse. A tentative request, such as "Would you mind . . ." gives the askee an open door to say no in a way that doesn't make it uncomfortable for either of you.

Never make a request a test of loyalty or friendship—if you need help in a major way, you could strain the limits of the relationship and be asking for a personal sacrifice that becomes more than a favor.

Don't make asking a favor a habit. The first time you ask for half a day off is within the realm of reasonable requests. Just because it was given readily does not mean you have carte blanche to ask for or take more time off at your whim. A favor once granted should not set a precedent or be something you expect to have repeated.

It goes without saying that thanks are in order for a favor given—immediate thanks.

If you are asked a favor, make no promises until you can be sure there won't be delays or obstacles in the way of your granting the favor. If you can't come through, you feel diminished and the favor-asker is disappointed. Instead, say "I'll see what I can do." This leaves you both a graceful out if what you can do is nothing at all.

Q. *Some of my co-workers are rather prejudiced, and very vocal about their opinions. I have to maintain a cordial working relationship even though I disagree with their sentiments and especially their comments. I'm* *new on the job but feel I need to say something. How should I handle the situation?*

A. If alone with someone who is voicing prejudice, you may quietly say "I don't go along with what you're saying" or "I don't like jokes that belittle people." If in a group where prejudiced statements are being made or jokes told, either try to change the subject or leave. Do not get into an argument or discussion.

Q. *I've seen my co-workers use drugs at work. Do I say something to them or to our supervisor?*

A. It is not really your place to say anything at all. Whistle-blowing is something to consider very carefully. Only if their job performance is impaired so that it affects you or clients adversely or if their using drugs jeopardizes the well-being or safety of others, should you consider saying something to your supervisor. Even then, you should choose your words judiciously, reporting that a client has complained to you about treatment received or that the lives or well-being of others are in danger. Accusations of drug use are very serious and, if unfounded, can have repercussions that affect not only the accused but you as well. Many companies have confidential treatment programs for employees with substance abuse or personal problems, and it is up to the supervisor to speak to the employee and to refer him or her for the program, not you.

Q. *On particularly bad days the boss has been known to fly off the handle and berate a staff member over an*

*inconsequential error—one we've all made at one time
or another. Should the boss apologize?*

A. Of course she should, just as she would when
losing her temper with friends or family. It is possible,
however, that she isn't even aware she is being overly
critical and is just reacting to pressure she is getting
from her boss. One of the best examples of this I have
seen was when the president of a company, upon
meeting a vice president in the hall, berated him for
the lateness of some report. The president moved on,
and the vice president, visibly upset, turned to one of
his staff members and yelled at him for no reason
perceivable to the assistant. The vice president
stomped out of the room, and the assistant was left
bewildered, angry, and looking for someone on
whom to vent his frustration.

The boss might never actually apologize for over-
reacting, although at a calmer moment he or she could
indicate, by a smile or kind word, that no harm was
intended (which is as close to an apology as you might
get). At times like this, it is helpful for co-workers to
support one another, again with a smile and kind
word, to show that they understand, that no one
should take a temporarily bad-tempered boss to heart,
and that they have all been there, at one time or
another.

Q. *I share my job with someone else. I am very neat
and leave our workspace ready for her when I leave. We
think the same way and the job goes smoothly, but she
leaves everything in a mess. She doesn't put files away,*

*leaves old coffee cups on the desk and the ashtray dirty.
I really mind coming in to her mess every day. How can
I say something to her without sounding petty?*

A. The next time you speak with her about some
aspect of a project, broach the subject as lightly as you
can. Say, "Working with you is like living with my old
roommate—she never emptied ashtrays or washed her
coffee cups either! Do you think you could clean up
before you leave? And while you're at it, could you
replace the files, too? It's easier for both of us to find
them if they get put back in place." If she says yes but
doesn't do it, try again. Say "Liz, you're smoking too
much. I counted your cigarette butts this morning.
You'd better start emptying the ashtray when you
leave, or I'm going to start worrying about your health
on the job." After two gentle tries, you have every
right to simply say, "Liz, please. Clean up before you
go. I hate walking in to your housekeeping chores
before I can get started working." You may begin to
feel like her mother, but you have a right to consideration that equals yours, and she has an obligation to
respond.

Q. *I frequently meet with others in their offices. I have
found that I am often left standing, holding my coat,
with no one offering to take it. Is there something I can
say?*

A. Yes. If no one takes your coat, just ask where to
hang it.

Q. *Sometimes I am kept waiting quite a while for an
appointment for which I am on time. How do I express
my frustration politely?*

A. Do not display your impatience by tapping your foot or looking obviously at your watch. If you are kept waiting over twenty minutes, say to the secretary, "Could you tell me when Mr. Genther will be free?" If you are unable to wait any longer, you may explain to the secretary and set up another appointment. Courtesy to the secretary, no matter how angry you are at her employer, is demanded.

Q. *If I am in someone's office and they receive a telephone call, what should I do?*
A. You may rise and softly ask, "Should I wait outside?" This gives the person the option of signalling you back to your chair if the call is not private and will be quick or responding, "Yes, thanks—I'll come get you as soon as I am finished."

Q. *I often hold meetings in my office. When my secretary is away from her desk, should I answer the telephone during a meeting or let it ring?*
A. There is something about a continually ringing telephone that is disruptive to people, so it is better not to let it ring and ring. You may answer the telephone, explaining immediately that you are in a meeting and promising to return the call at your earliest convenience. To save this interruption, you can have your secretary ask someone else to cover her desk while she is away, ask the switchboard to hold your calls, or put your calls on call forwarding, if your office is equipped with it, to forward your calls to another office where messages may be taken for you.

Q. *We just moved to a larger more formal space. Visitors are announced at the receptionist in the lobby who calls the office to announce their arrival and then sends them to the right floor. Should I meet my visitors at the elevator, or may I have my secretary do it?*

A. Either you or your secretary may wait by the elevator to escort your visitor to your office. If it is your secretary, he or she would say, "Dr. Farnham? I'm Ann Goering, Mrs. Neilsen's secretary. Won't you please come with me and I'll take you to her office." Your secretary can then take the visitor's coat and ask him to be seated while she announces his arrival or escort him directly into your office if you are ready for him.

If you meet him yourself and haven't been introduced before, you would say, "Dr. Farnham? Hi, I'm Greta Nielsen. It's so nice to meet you. Come on back to the office."

What is important is that one of you be there so he is not left to wander around by himself or to try to find you on his own.

Q. *When I have a business visitor, is it necessary to introduce him to anyone we pass in the corridor?*

A. No, it is not. Should someone stop by your office while he is meeting with you, you should make a brief introduction; or if you are taking him on a tour of the department, you may or may not introduce him, depending on whether you are stopping at each work station for lengthy explanations of the function of that area. This gives him an opportunity to ask a question directly of the person whose office or work space it is and is more polite than pretending the person in that office is invisible. Otherwise, it is pointless to introduce him to everyone who passes you since they would have no reason to speak to one another.

Q. *Who should terminate an appointment when the business at hand is finished? The person whose office it is or the visitor?*

A. Normally, both parties know when the business discussion is finished and rise simultaneously, shake hands, and part. If this doesn't occur, then the host should say, "I think that wraps it up—is there anything else we need to talk about before you go?" If there is, that business is conducted and then the host says, "Thank you so much for coming—let me see you out, and I'll be back in touch soon."

If the visitor feels the appointment is dragging on pointlessly and the host is making no move to end the meeting, then the visitor can say, "Sam, thank you so much for all your time. This has been a productive meeting, and I'll be on my way. I will talk to you soon." This person should then rise, shake hands, and leave.

Q. *How should bad news be delivered in a business environment?*

A. Preferably, as personally as possible. Manners, as well as human decency, dictate that sensitivity and professionalism be combined when bad news must be delivered. A curt "you're fired" notice enclosed with a paycheck is neither sensitive nor professional.

If across-the-board cutbacks must occur, the department head should call a department staff meeting, review what is happening throughout the company, and then immediately schedule individual appointments with every employee, both those who are being let go and those who are not. For the former, he can use this time to explain termination benefits, if any, and to offer help in the employee's job search. For the latter, a brief personal meeting serves to reassure them and to restore some sense of morale.

In the case of an individual job termination, as hard as it may be, the supervisor should meet with the employee, discuss why the decision was made, offer constructive suggestions, and review the terms of severance.

If the bad news has to do with a death or tragedy occurring to someone in the company, again it is important for the news to be communicated directly rather than on paper. This helps to diminish rumors and anxieties and reinforces the human side of management.

Office Romance Dos and Don'ts

Q. *I have been seeing a lot of one of my co-workers. He is separated from his wife, and I am single. How can we keep our relationship from becoming the target of office gossip?*

A. Keep your social and your office lives separate. To avoid speculation, don't have frequent lunches together or leave or arrive at the office together. During working hours, avoid touching, lengthy eye contact, or giving the appearance of shared secrets and other suggestive actions. In short, behave in a friendly manner, as you did before you began your relationship, never in an intimate manner.

Q. *I am a private secretary and I am afraid my boss and I are becoming emotionally involved. How can we handle this in order to protect his position—and mine?*

A. Whether either or both of you are married or not, you are both jeopardizing your jobs if you allow your relationship to affect your work. If you feel that you cannot continue to work closely together and still maintain a professional attitude, then you might consider asking for a transfer to another department or seeking another job. Because of his position, it would be easier for you to seek a transfer than it would be for him. Your public reason for requesting a change has to be a professional one—a new challenge, a new interest, an opportunity for growth—and needs his support with management or personnel so that it does not appear to be for personal reasons.

Q. *At an out-of town restaurant one evening recently, I saw my boss sitting in a corner with one of the stenographers from the office. I think he knows that I saw him, but he has not mentioned it. Should I say anything to him or just let it pass?*

A. Let it pass. Although he may be mixing his personal life with his professional one, what he, or she, does during out-of-the-office hours is not open for discussion. There may be an innocent explanation, and by bringing it up, even just to say "Isn't that a great restaurant?" would imply that you thought he was "guilty." To discuss it with others would be to gossip and to create unwarranted speculation, and to discuss it with him would be prying. If he mentions it to you or tries to explain, accept what he says, make a neutral comment about enjoying that particular restaurant, and drop it. From a practical point of view, your discussing his actions, either with him or others, could lead to possible resentment on his part and a lost job for you.

Q. *Two of my co-workers have been having a relationship outside the office. They have been fairly discreet about it at work, but they just broke up and the woman* *keeps talking to me about it and asking me what she should do. What should I do?*

A. Since she seems to consider you a friend and to want to talk to you about her problems, you certainly should listen, but do not take sides. You still have to work with both of them and really cannot afford to become part of someone else's office romance. Don't give other than general advice, and don't get trapped into serving as a mediator between the two of them. Not only does this interfere with business, but if they should get back together, both of them, unfairly, will resent your knowing all about their difficulties, a situation that can have an impact on your future working relationship with either of them.

Q. *Several of us have lunch together frequently, and often the topic of conversation is the romantic life of one or the other in the group. I have felt uncomfortable sharing that aspect of my personal life with them, but wonder if I should.*

A. No, you shouldn't. The last thing you need is to have co-workers, even though they are work "friends," be in a position of knowing all about your private life. Should you be promoted over them, they could use that information in a negative way against you, and should one of them be promoted over you, the same thing could happen, jeopardizing your own job status. You don't need to feel you have to exchange a confidence for having received one of theirs and can stay noncommital when asked direct questions. Simply saying "You all have much more exciting lives than mine!" or "There's nobody really special in my life right now, although I have a lot of friends I enjoy spending time with" (even if you are passionately in love) should keep them from pursuing you for details and should keep your private life where it belongs—away from the office.

Q. *I've been offered a transfer to a department where my former lover works. Our relationship is definitely over, but I'm not sure if this is a good idea.*
A. The answer to your dilemma depends not only on your feelings but his as well. Call him and ask if you can speak to him for a few minutes. Be frank. Tell him you would really like the job, but don't want your past relationship to interfere. If you think you will have no problem working closely with him, say so, and see if he feels the same way. If he does, you should be comfortable accepting the transfer. If he doesn't think it will work out, you probably should consider turning down the opportunity, since his attitude can be an obstacle, in many subtle ways, to your success in a new job.

Q. *Everybody is talking about my boss and his secretary. They've been seen together outside the office several times. Should I tell him?*
A. That totally depends on your relationship with him. Even if you have a close and open relationship, he still could resent your bringing the subject up. On the other hand, he might appreciate your alerting him to the fact that what he thought was confidential is the

subject of the office rumor mill. The general rule is mind your own business. He obviously knows what he is doing and the risk he is taking.

Q. *My boss gets a lot of calls from his girlfriend, and they seem to have a rather combative relationship. He tends to shout over the telephone when he is fighting with her, and the entire office can hear him. Should I say something?*

A. You may, but you may also just get up and close his office door when this occurs. Part of your job is to protect him in situations like this, and this would be more discreet than discussing it with him. If he asks you why you keep shutting his door, you should explain, saying that you thought he may not be aware that his voice carried outside his office and that you thought he might prefer privacy.

Q. *Two people in our office are engaged to be married, which seems to be fine with management, but they act like they are at home. They kiss each other good-bye if one is going to a meeting, and they are always touching. How should the rest of us handle this?*

A. You shouldn't. Just ignore it unless their behavior is so offensive that something needs to be said. If it is, then a gentle, "Hey, you two, save that for home!" serves as a reminder that they are making a public display of their affection. Otherwise, it is really up to management to address the issue privately with the two of them.

Business Travel Etiquette

Q. *I'm a junior staff member and will be traveling on business for the first time soon. Have you any suggestions?*

A. The first rule is that a junior executive defers to a senior executive. This means you are the one to sit on the jump seat in the taxi or limousine, or in the middle seat of the car or plane. Other suggestions include the following:

- Keep scrupulous records of your expenses. The IRS has standards and guidelines for what are and are not acceptable business expenses.
- Keep luggage light. Don't expect anyone else to carry it for you.
- Allow for travel fatigue. Plan to arrive early and leave time to rest. Don't book a dinner meeting if you will be traveling all afternoon or you run the risk of being sleepy and not at your best.
- If you use someone's office during your stay in another city, leave a gift as thanks.

Q. *I will be traveling on a corporate plane for several hours. How are refreshments handled? Will I be served lunch, or should I take my own on board?*

A. Corporate travel is much more informal than commercial travel. Generally, corporate planes have a kitchenette area where food is set up by the crew. You are expected to help yourself unless there is a steward on board. The crew usually instructs passengers and tells them what is available, but their job is to fly the plane not to serve. If this is the case, you go to the food service area when you are ready, take your meal back to your seat, and dispose of the remains afterward. It is not polite to leave your refuse for the captain to clean up for you.

Q. *When I fly privately, who carries my bags on and off the plane?*
A. You do. The pilot and co-pilot may offer to assist, and if there is a flight attendant on board, he or she will help you stow it away once on board. But it is expected that you do the carrying.

Q. *When flying privately, who boards first, my boss or me?*
A. If you arrive together, your boss boards first. If you arrive ahead of him or her, however, board as you arrive. There is no need to stand on the runway inhaling aircraft exhaust waiting for your boss. However, if you are not the senior person, take either the seat you are shown by the crew or one to the rear, leaving the more forward seats for those senior to you.

Q. *Do I tip the pilot or crew on a corporate or other private plane?*
A. Tips are not in order if the plane is owned and staffed by the corporation or owned by the corpora-

tion and staffed by a management firm. Tips are given to the crew of chartered planes. The highest-ranking person gives the gratuity on behalf of your party rather than each of you lining up and giving individual tips.

Q. *How should I dress when traveling on business?*
A. Dress as though you were going to the office. You are traveling on behalf of the company and therefore dress to represent it.

Q. *Who picks up the check at dinner out of town?*
A. No matter who picks up the check, the company pays the bill. Even so, certain protocol is followed. When a superior is traveling with a lower-level executive, whether male or female, the higher-ranking one is expected to pay. However, when it is a small amount for a drink or snack, the lower-ranking employee may properly say "I'll get it" and do so. If both travelers are of equal rank, they may split bills as they go or each pick up checks on alternate days.

When being entertained by people from a company office you are visiting, it is expected that they pick up the check, although there may be exceptions to this rule—instances of specific company policy, for example. You may certainly host your host at dinner if you are staying for several days and having several meals together—in fact, you should. But check with your bookkeeping or accounting department for any regulations regarding who will be reimbursed for what.

Q. *When two co-workers travel outside their office, who pays if they travel by taxi? Who drives if they travel by car?*

A. If both have expense accounts and either one would be reimbursed for the fare, it matters not at all who pays. When traveling by car, the owner or the renter of the car usually drives. When the owner is not familiar with the area, however, and the associate is, the driver may certainly ask the associate to do the driving. If both are from out of town, who drives is a toss-up. On a long trip, driving duty is shared.

Q. *We have a company chauffeur, and I will soon be using him as transportation to and from meetings. Do I sit in front with him or in the back? Do I talk to him? Do I wait for him to open the door for me?*

A. It is expected that you sit in the back of the car. If you are traveling with senior executives and you are the junior member, you would sit in front if there wasn't enough space for all of you to sit comfortably in the back. You may exchange greetings, but it is not necessary for you to carry on a running conversation unless you want to. Rules about who opens the door have relaxed in the past few years. There is no reason you cannot let yourself out of the car when you reach your destination instead of sitting and waiting for him to come around the car to open the door for you, unless you need assistance or he has already jumped out to assist you, in which case you would wait for him. Just say, "Thanks, Lonnie. I'll be finished in about an hour and will look for you here," and get out of the car.

Q. *When I travel for my company, I have to take quite a lot of equipment in addition to my suitcase. If I use an airport porter to help me, how much should I tip him?*

A. Fifty cents to one dollar per bag and piece of equipment is standard. If he tags your luggage and delivers it to the check-in desk, you would tip him at the time he takes your bags from you since you won't see him later. If he is going to follow you with your luggage to the boarding area, then you would tip him after your arrival at the gate.

International Business Etiquette

Q. *I work in the headquarters of a large international company. We have many visitors from our foreign subsidiaries whose customs are different from ours, and I will soon begin extensive travel on business to their offices. Can you give me any guidelines about etiquette in other countries?*

A. There are several overall guidelines that apply to international travel. For specific pointers on particular countries, call or write that country's embassy or consulate. Most of them have printed material for business visitors or can answer your questions. There are also country-specific travel books available at public libraries, with cultural, business, and general travel tips for the business traveler. They have been written by people who have spent years conducting business in these countries and can be invaluable to a corporate person planning to travel and work internationally.

Examples of things that it would be important to know and that could make or break your transaction are the following:

- If you are invited to dine at a Saudi Arabian's home, a gift is appropriate and appreciated, but never a gift of food, which would indicate that you did not expect to dine well. Flowers, books, or a United States souvenir are welcome, but never anything made of leather that might be pigskin. Never take a gift for your host's wife, but gifts for his children, boys or girls, are appropriate.

- Body language is key when doing business in Saudi Arabia. Saudis tend to stand quite close to you when they speak. Do not back away or you will appear to be rebuffing the speaker. Additionally, hand gestures are considered impolite, as are the soles of your shoes. Never cross your legs so the bottoms of your shoes show.

- Never throw back your head and laugh uproariously at a joke told by your Japanese counterpart. It is very gauche to show the inside of your mouth. Even if you are a six-foot-four former linebacker, cover your mouth with your hand to laugh.

- Keep in mind that "face," or honor, is still very much a part of the Japanese culture and do nothing to cause your business counterpart or host to lose his. This means do not haggle over price. Generally, to cause a Japanese businessman to compromise implies that he has lost something, and usually his first offer is close to what he wants to pay. Also, do not give a gift of greater value than the one he gives you.

- In China, the law prohibits individual business persons from accepting personal gifts. The gift

must be to the organization as a whole. Don't ever give a clock, which symbolizes death.
- Never give a gift of cowhide in India, where the cow is sacred.

In general:

- Before you leave on a trip, try to learn how to say please and thank you in that country's native language.
- Always show appreciation for the culture, music, and art of the country you are visiting.
- Scrupulously respect your host's dietary customs, holidays, religion, and form of government. Don't make comparisons unless asked, and even then, not in a judgmental way.
- Keep in mind that business is more formal in all other countries than it is in the United States and Canada, and conduct yourself accordingly. Correspondence is also more formal.
- Be prompt.
- Apologize for your lack of proficiency in your host's language.
- Always be well groomed. Women should wear conservative dresses, skirts, or suits, never pants, nor should they wear sleeveless tops or very short skirts.
- Shaking hands is very important in Europe. In some countries, women still do not shake hands, however, so wait for them to extend a hand to you if you aren't sure. In many countries, women are not as much a part of the

business world as we are accustomed to. When they are, they tend to practice social manners instead of business manners.

- Be courteous and respectful at all times and never do anything that would offend your host's pride.

Q. *I was told not to acknowledge the presence of a woman in Saudi Arabia. I find this hard to believe. Is this true?*

A. Yes. As alien as it may seem to you, when a Saudi is accompanied by a woman, do not even notice that she exists unless he introduces her.

Q. *Is business in most countries conducted from 9 to 5 as it is in the United States?*

A. No. In many European countries, businesses close down at lunchtime. In northern France, for example, the business day is usually 8:30 A.M. to 12:30 P.M., and then from 3:00 P.M. to 6:30 P.M. It is important that you investigate the business customs and working hours of the companies with which you will be conducting business so that you can be sure to plan appropriately and leave enough time to accomplish your business. Naturally, our 9 to 5 changes as time zones change, and it is logical to adjust your schedule accordingly.

Q. *Sometimes I have difficulty understanding when my host in another country speaks. He is speaking slowly, for my benefit, so I don't want to embarrass him, but what should I do?*

A. Be as charming as you can, apologize for your own limitations, and ask him to repeat what he has just said. More harm can be done by your nodding and smiling and pretending you know what he is saying than by asking him to repeat a statement.

Q. *When traveling to another country on business, who is responsible for entertaining, me or my host from that country?*
A. Your host is responsible for entertaining you initially, but in some countries it is expected that you will reciprocate the entertainment while there. It is important that your entertaining be equal to but never more lavish in style than theirs.

Q. *I am going to Switzerland on business. I want to take pictures to bring back and show my family. Is this appropriate?*
A. It's fine on your off hours, but not when you are conducting business. You are not a tourist, you are representing your firm as a business person. The camera should never accompany you to a business meeting or other function.

Q. *When in England on business, I am frequently entertained at functions where the national anthem is played. Do I remain seated or stand for this?*
A. Always stand and show respect for your host country's anthem.

Q. *I am going to close a business deal in another country. I don't speak their language, and they don't speak English. What should I do?*

A. It is best if you hire an interpreter. This should not offend the company executives with whom you are doing business and will, in most cases, facilitate your communicating with one another. They may provide their own interpreter, as well.

Q. *I will be traveling to several European and Mideast countries on business. What kind of wardrobe should I plan?*

A. You should pack professional business clothing that is appropriate to the climate. For men, conservative business suits and ties are best. If you know you will be entertained formally, a tuxedo should be packed, as well. For after-hours or informal entertainments, sport jackets, slacks, and lightweight sweaters are generally appropriate. Your appearance and grooming should show respect to your host and host country and should reflect your status as a business person. If traveling to the Mideast during the hot seasons when the temperature can travel over 100 degrees, lightweight suits are a must. Follow your host's cues as to whether or not to remove your jacket. Do not do it if he does not.

For women, conservative is again the key word. No backless, sleeveless, or strapless dresses for business. Mid- or long-sleeved dresses are best, and classic pumps are more suitable than toeless or backless shoes. Dresses with jackets or suits are perfect. Blouses should be buttoned more to the top than not, and jewelry should not be ostentatious. As in your own office, keep perfume to a pleasant scent, not an overwhelming blast. Make-up should be light, and hair should be smooth and neat. For evening entertainment, dresses that can be dressed up with a change of accessories are easiest for traveling, and a long gown is not necessary except for balls and the most formal parties.

It would be unusual for a woman to travel to Mideast countries on business, where women are not a major part of the workforce, but if you should be heading that way, lightweight dresses and suits will be the most comfortable. Arms must be covered, and necklines buttoned to the top. Short, short skirts and pants are not appropriate.

Q. *How do I arrange for transportation in the countries I will be visiting on business?*
A. Talk to your travel agent or corporate travel department about what you think your needs will be. He or she can make arrangements for you. If you are not using a travel agent and feel you will want a car at your disposal, talk to American car rental agencies with international divisions. If you find you have need of ground transportation after you arrive, the hotel concierge would be your most helpful resource in finding cars, drivers, or taxis.

Q. *I will be entertaining clients in several countries abroad but don't know anything about how to find restaurants. What should I do?*
A. Preferably, arrive a day or two early so you can shop around. It is best to be as prepared as possible, and there are now many excellent magazines and

guides for frequent flyers and travelers available which review restaurants and dinner clubs. If your local library does not subscribe to them, ask your travel agent if she or he can loan you copies or, better yet, make recommendations for the cities in which you will be entertaining. You do not want to be at a disadvantage or have to ask your guests where you should take them. This would be awkward for them, not knowing what price range or style of restaurant you had in mind. When you are the host, you want to be as in control as possible. This includes being comfortable with the selection of the place, knowing the menu choices, and being assured that you will have selected an environment in which you can conduct business and entertain socially in the style befitting your needs that is also complementary to your guests' needs.

Q. *If I need to send faxes back to my office, may I ask my international business associate to use his?*
A. No, you may not. Nor should you ask for secretarial services or make international calls from his telephone, unless your associate is in a branch office of your company. You should never charge your host from an unrelated company with your office costs. Most large, international hotels are now equipped with fax equipment. You should use your hotel telephone for your calls. If the time change is such that you need to place calls from someone's office and not travel back to your hotel, then you should charge your calls to your own office or to yourself on an international credit card. Secretarial services are harder to

come by. If the concierge cannot help you, you may, as a last resort, ask your host if he can recommend someone. He will most likely offer his own staff to assist you. If this is the case, it is important that you thank the secretary who types for you or performs other secretarial services by giving her a gift or flowers and that you thank your host profusely for providing you with this help.

Q. *Is it appropriate for my office in the States to send me faxes or call me at the offices of European clients when I am there in meetings?*
A. Yes. Because of the time change and because immediate replies are often necessary, it is acceptable for your office to contact you at someone else's office. Naturally, you should not monopolize anyone's office or keep your clients waiting while you conduct other business for extraordinary amounts of time.

Leaving Your Job

Q. *I'm displeased with my assistant's performance. How do I handle the situation?*
A. Before you do anything, check with your personnel department on what the company procedure is for reprimanding an employee or putting someone on warning. If yours is a union situation, you also must check with the union contract terms for procedures.

In general, not including various company policies on this topic, it is incumbent upon you to meet with your assistant, in private, and review those areas of his performance that are displeasing to you. It is possible that you have overlooked certain areas of training or information sharing with him, and he is unaware of what is expected of him. Be clear. Don't just say "I'm not happy with your work." Ask him how he feels about his job and about how he is accomplishing it. Tell him those areas that you feel need improvement, and why. Ask him if he understands what you expect, and then follow up by telling him precisely what your expectations are and how you want them to be carried out. Ask for his opinion on what you have just said. In this way, you can better understand whether he is an overall poor performer or whether he will do well now that he has direction from you. Then follow up two weeks later in another private appointment. If he has improved, reinforce his improvement and tell him. If he has not, put him on warning that he still is not performing according to expectations for the job, and that he has another two weeks to shape up. At the end of the second two weeks, you have to either commend him for his improvement or suggest that he look for another job. If possible, tell him those areas of his work that are good or excellent. This not only is courteous but helps rebuild his morale.

Q. *I'm not happy with a recent performance review. How do I bring up the subject with my boss?*
A. You should have been informed, at the time you were hired, what company policy is on your rights during a performance review. If you were not, or if you are unclear, check with personnel for procedures you may follow. If you belong to a union, check with your shop steward as to what recourse you have and how you are to proceed. If your company does not have a personnel department and a union situation is not involved, then you have to speak up. Very often, a poor performance review is based on a complete misunderstanding of what is actually expected of you and what you believed those expectations to be.

If your boss has expressed displeasure with specific aspects of your job performance, request an appointment and explain to her why you have performed the way you have, what you thought the expectations were, and that you thought you were doing what she wanted. This is an opportunity to clear up any misunderstandings. Whether you intend to continue in your present job or to look elsewhere, it is important that you go on record with your point of view.

Most job performance evaluations include paperwork with space for your supervisor to list your pluses and minuses, and a space for you to react. It is important for the future, whether within the same company or outside it, that you not only record your reactions but that you verbalize them to your boss. She is someone you need as a reference if you look for a new job, and for your own sake you have to make her understand what you perceive versus what she perceives.

Q. *I've received a job offer that I'm thrilled about. What is the proper way to quit my present job?*
A. It is incredibly thoughtless and poor form to out and out quit without giving notice. Even though a company can fire you with no notice, it behooves you to be as cooperative as possible in giving notice so that you can always return to the company with good will on all sides, and so that you are sure to receive a good reference should you ever be job hunting again.

Depending on the level of your job, a letter of resignation should be submitted. Ideally, you should request an appointment with your supervisor so you can verbally express your appreciation for the job you are leaving, as well as for him or for her, and so you can explain why you are making the move. At that time, submit your letter of resignation. Explain that your move is because of an opportunity for advancement, if that is the case, or for a career shift, if that is your reason for changing. Even if you have sought a new job because you hate your boss, you needn't say so. It is not a good idea to slam doors behind you as you go—you never know when you might need a reference or want to return to the company in a different capacity—or to a job where your boss might also be several years hence.

Nothing could be worse than to seek a new job in the future, only to find that the person you have told you have no respect for and can't work for another moment is in a position of authority in the new company. It is a smaller-than-ever world, and there is no reason, except for personal satisfaction, to burn your bridges behind you. You may need to cross them again someday.

Q. *My boss seems angry that I'm leaving this job for another position in the company. How do I handle his anger?*

A. Try to evaluate why he is angry. It could be that he takes your leaving personally. It could also be that he feels he has invested considerable time training you and that, by leaving, you have wasted his time. Whatever his reasons for anger, you must not react in kind. Request an appointment, ask him why he seems angry, and explain that your reasons for leaving have entirely to do with your career future. Thank him profusely for the opportunities he has given you. Part of business etiquette is consideration for the feelings of those with whom you work, and it would serve you well to try to determine his and to assuage any negative thoughts he is having.

Q. *How do you look for a new job while keeping your present one?*
A. Quietly. Don't confide in your best office friend, who will very likely want to confide your news in someone else. You don't want management to hear of your job hunt from anyone but you.

Most companies understand the need for confidentiality and will not call your boss for a reference without asking you first or until you are a serious candidate for the job. It would be a good idea to say that you have not informed your company that you are looking, so they won't call. They also understand that your time for interviewing is limited to lunch hours and before and after work. It is not correct to take extra, paid time away from your current company to job hunt.

When you are offered a job, you must go immediately to your supervisor and tell him, letting him know the amount of notice you are giving, depending on your longevity with the company and your job title; two weeks is customary.

Q. *Several times I've been asked for a reference for employees who have been fired. How should I handle this?*
A. First, be open-minded and realize the good qualities the employee has. Emphasize these. Explain that

although the employee was unable to perform as expected in your company's position, he has certain strengths, which could be well applied somewhere else. Second, be tactful. Employees are no longer prohibited from seeing the letters of reference in their files, and what you write could trigger a lawsuit. Avoid making sweeping statements of condemnation or drawing unwarranted conclusions. The safest way to write a negative reference is to say as little as possible but make it clear to the prospective employer that you will be glad to answer any questions about the person on the telephone. If you prefer not to write a letter of reference, for whatever reason, simply decline the request to do so.

Q. *How do you decline to write a letter of reference?*
A. Just say that you are unable to write the letter and offer instead that your telephone number be given to those requesting a letter of reference. If you do receive a call, again accentuate the positive without dwelling on the negative, simply saying that although the job with you did not work out, you feel the person's strengths could make a contribution in another job.

Q. *How do you write a letter of reference for an employee you're sorry to lose?*
A. Preferably, you would write a letter of reference to a specific company, at the request of the departing employee rather than a "To Whom It May Concern" letter. An example of a positive letter is:

Dear Mr. Johnson:

It is a pleasure to recommend Samantha Freeman to you. During her five years with our company she was an asset to the department and was instrumental in determining several cost-effective procedures that benefited the company greatly. Her supervisors and co-workers continually praised her work and her ability to identify problems and propose solutions.

While we are saddened by her decision to relocate, we know she will be a valued employee to any firm fortunate enough to have her in its employ.

Sincerely, [etc.]

Q. *I changed jobs within the same corporation. My former boss told my replacement to call me with questions. The first week I didn't mind, but now it's starting to interfere with my new position. How can I put an end to it?*

A. Call your former boss and explain that, as much as you want to continue to help, you are running out of hours in the day. Suggest that your boss, your replacement, and you meet for lunch to go over a final list of their questions, after which you really have to concentrate on your new job. Naturally assure them that you are not becoming incommunicado, but that you won't be able to respond as quickly and feel this will be an excellent way to complete the training you have been giving.

Q. *What is the proper form for telling someone with whom you are interviewing that your current employer* *doesn't know you are looking for a new job (so that she isn't called for a reference)?*

A. Simply say so. Generally, an interviewer will ask you that question to preclude an ill-timed reference call. If you are not asked, however, and if you believe you will be considered seriously for the job, you may say, "My company does not know I am looking, so I would appreciate it if you would not call them for a reference unless I am the candidate you would select for this job. I would like to be the one to tell my boss I have interviewed with you before you call her.

Usually, a potential employer will ask you for references. Assuming you have asked those you list for permission, you might suggest that the interviewer feel free to check with them while considering your candidacy.

Q. *How can I be sure the people who have agreed to serve as references for me aren't becoming annoyed by too many calls?*

A. There are two things you can do. The first is to ask a potential employer not to check your references unless you are being seriously considered for the job, explaining that you do not wish them to be bothered too frequently.

The second is, if your job search is proving to be a lengthy one, to check back with those who have agreed to give you a recommendation to make sure they are still willing, explaining that you are concerned that too much of their time is being taken.

Q. *I have been approached by a "head hunter" to discuss a new job, although I wasn't really looking.*

What exactly is a "head hunter," and is there anything I should know about what would be expected of me?

A. "Head hunter" is a slang phrase for an executive recruiter or executive placement firm, which is like an employment agency but usually only conducts a search for an executive level person. Executive recruiters are retained by a corporation to find qualified candidates for specific positions. They read the business press and work from recommendations made by other executives and from their own contacts. Your name could have been passed on by an associate, co-worker, or client.

An executive recruiter will want to meet with you, at your convenience, to get to know you, your capabilities, and goals. The first meeting is usually lengthy since the recruiter wants to recommend only people who are most qualified for a particular job and whose personality, appearance, conduct, etc. is of the caliber he or she will feel comfortable recommending.

He or she may invite you to a meeting in his or her office, or to lunch or dinner. The recruiter picks up the tab, not you, nor should you offer to do so. You should have a current resumé with you and be prepared for the inspection of your life. Your manners, attitude, appearance, and work experience will be closely scrutinized, just as they would be by a corporate or personnel officer were your interview to be with a company. As with any other interview, it is appropriate for you to write a thank-you note to the recruiter, subsequent to your first meeting.

If you find that the job he or she describes to you (and it is likely you will not be told the name of the company at your first meeting) is not one in which you are interested, you may certainly say so, but ask that the recruiter keep you in mind for other opportunities as they arise, explaining what you would be interested in. When you do decide to launch a new job campaign, you may get back in touch with the recruiter to tell him or her and follow up with a letter, enclosing an updated resumé.

Q. *What are interim executive placement firms? Are there any particular rules for meeting with them?*
A. These are firms that specialize in placing executives in temporary positions. For example, if a company is beginning a new division and needs an experienced person to set it up but doesn't plan to keep the person once the department is launched, that company would need an interim executive. The personnel companies that specialize in this kind of placement are called interim placement firms.

The rules for meeting with them are the same as those for meeting with an executive recruiter. If you get in touch with them and not the other way around, you would send a letter explaining that you are interested in interim work, highlighting certain areas of professional experience that would lend themselves to interim work. You would enclose a resumé and follow up with a telephone call a week later. You would not invite a recruiter to lunch or dinner but would request a meeting at his or her office. If he or she invites you to meet in a restaurant, he or she pays the bill, not you. Interim executive recruiters are interested only in those people who really are looking for long- or short-term interim positions, not in someone who is looking for a full-time job, so it is not cricket to take an interim position and leave it because a full-time one is offered in the middle of an interim project.

Q. *When my company was in recent financial trouble, several people quit for other jobs. One person in particular walked through the departments on his last day saying, "I hate to be the rat who is leaving the sinking ship." I thought this was rude and derogatory to the rest of us, but it made me wonder what one does say when leaving a job. Do you have any advice?*
A. You are correct in that your former associate was rude in his statement. What one says is a warm good-bye, with a thank-you to everyone for the pleasure of working with them. No matter how glad one may be to be leaving, one should never express it to those left behind.

Q. *I was fired from my last job during a large lay-off. I wanted to say good-bye to a lot of associates but was too embarrassed that I had been fired and didn't know what to say. How should I have handled this?*
A. Unless you are fired for some criminal act or for extremely unprofessional behavior, there is nothing to be embarrassed about, and it is a shame not to be able to bid farewell to those who have been working associates. What you say is, "I have just been given notice and wanted you to know how very much I have

enjoyed working with you and that I will miss you."
To those with whom you would like to stay in touch,
you say so, making sure they have a telephone number
where they can reach you.

What you do not say are negative words about
the company, your boss, or the situation. You do not
complain, nor do you gossip, nor do you try to justify
what happened. You should not be embarrassed if you
become a little teary, which only shows that you care
about the people you are leaving. Others may not
know what to say to you since they will be having
mixed feelings of gladness that it is you, not them, and
of sadness because they are sorry to see you go. What
they should say is, "Joe, I am really sorry that this
happened. Not having you here will be a real loss, and
I will miss you. Thanks for stopping by."

Q. *What should I say to co-workers when I quit a job
for another one?*
A. You say only that your new job is an opportunity
you couldn't refuse. You do not run through a list of
why you are choosing to leave, nor do you bad-mouth
the company or any of its employees. Even if you were
miserably unhappy, there is no reason to use this time
as a forum to be negative about your former boss or
any of your co-workers. You have to realize that the
people you are saying this to are staying and that they
don't really want to hear that they are foolish not to
be leaving because it is such a terrible place. If you
really have strong negative comments to make that
you feel will help the company in the future, save

them for an exit interview with your boss or the personnel department and spare your co-workers. You do not need to demean the company or anyone in it to make yourself and your new opportunity look better.

Q. *What is the proper way to conduct myself during an exit interview?*
A. With composure, decorum, and professionalism. What you say will be noted in your file, and others, and you, do not want to leave on a wave of bad feelings or bad impressions. You also don't want your file to be closed on a sour note since you may want to ask for a reference some time in the future. If your situation was not a pleasurable one and you have constructive comments to make, by all means make them. If you did not get along with your boss, you can say it was a matter of a personality conflict. If pressed, you may cite a few examples of that conflict, explaining that you just did not find it a positive atmosphere for you. You should end the interview with a positive comment about someone or some aspect of the job you are leaving and thank the interviewer for his or her time. If you truly are leaving because of a better opportunity, say so. Say, "I feel I have grown a lot here, but this new opportunity will give me the chance to grow more and to add another dimension to my resumé."

Exit interviews are conducted for two reasons: One, to debrief you if there is information you have that should not be shared outside and two, to ascertain if there is a problem which was not known previously. You should not say, "Just ask Larry—he'll tell you what it's like up there!" to strengthen your statement. Larry can speak for himself if and when he wants to, and your comments should be kept to your own situation and the reason for your departure.

Especially for Women

Q. *Several of the men in our office insist on calling the women "honey," "sweetie," etc. We resent it but have said nothing because we are afraid of jeopardizing our jobs. What can we do?*
A. You should speak up. The next time this happens, say "My name is Mary, not honey." Keep repeating it—perhaps at least some of the men will change their ways.

Q. *Should a woman stand when a man enters her office?*
A. Yes, if the man entering is a superior, an older person, a client or a customer, or anyone she is meeting for the first time from inside or outside the company. She does not stand for a male co-worker or a male secretary or assistant.

Q. *Is there anything about manners I should know when traveling to our international offices?*
A. You should recognize that most businessmen from other countries use social manners during business hours. You should not have this be the time to assert your equality rights, which could be offensive to them. Instead, graciously accept their offer to assist

you with your coat, hold the door for you, or rise every time you enter the room. Accepting their use of manners really is part of doing business with them.

Q. *I am relatively young and one of the few women executives in my office. The men insist on treating me like I was a piece of fragile china, and I resent it. What should I say to them?*

A. Absolutely nothing at all. It is important to acknowledge that older executives have had to go through some, for them, radical changes just in having women peers in the office. Out of habit, they will use social manners, and you should not be offended by this or speak to them about it. Continue being self-sufficient, but not to the point of belligerence, which will not further your cause. What is important is that you are given and take the opportunity to perform your professional responsibilities as you wish, not that someone insists on helping you carry a carton of software accessories to your office.

Q. *How should I handle vulgar language spoken by my male counterparts?*

A. By not making a federal case out of it. An elegantly raised eyebrow, an "I beg your pardon?" or a repetition of their statement ("Let's go over the last * quarterly report to make sure there aren't any * * overbudget situations") without the vulgarities ("Let me be sure I understand . . . you want to review the last quarterly report for any unusual overbudget situations . . .") indicates that you are less than pleased with expletives that could readily be deleted. Vulgar language is out of place, particularly in the office, and your point will be made without your saying "Please don't talk like that in front of me," which makes the statement that you want to be treated like a woman, not like a co-worker. Under no circumstances should you fall in with unprofessional language habits just to show you are really "one of the guys."

Q. *I have an almost all-male staff. When I take one of my assistants out to lunch, he gets uncomfortable when the bill arrives and always offers to pay. What should I say to him?*
A. Just explain that you appreciate his courtesy but that it is company policy that a business lunch is picked up by the senior person.

Q. *Invariably, my boss introduces me as "the prettiest senior vice president in the company." Everyone (but me) chuckles appreciatively, since I am the only female executive at that level. How can I get him to stop?*
A. If you have a fairly decent working relationship with him, tackle the problem the next time you lunch or at the end of a business discussion. Say "Alex, I appreciate your nice comments about my appearance, but when you introduce me [that way], I feel it puts the focus on the way I look, not on what I am doing for the company or saying at the meeting. I've noticed you never introduce Barry as 'the most handsome executive vice president in the company.' I need your help supporting our projects, and I really feel that singling me out this way takes away from the support we could get from everyone else. What do you think?"

Q. *I have a close friend in my office who has received several promotions. There are a lot of snide comments by some of the men about how she has made her way to the top, which simply aren't true. How can I defend her character and stop this gossip? Should I tell her what people are saying?*

A. The next time comments are made in your hearing, you may say words to the effect of, "Glenn, you know that isn't true! Sarah has worked harder than the rest of us put together to earn her promotions. She's lucky to be pretty as well as terrific at her job, but that doesn't mean you have the right to talk about her that way." or "You guys are setting yourselves up for one big slander lawsuit if you keep this up. There is no basis except jealousy for your mean comments. You know that Sarah is a lovely person and has earned every bit of the credit she's received, so cut it out!" This may not stop the gossip totally, but it will make several of the participants think twice before they utter their defamatory remarks out loud again.

Since she is a close friend, you should tell her what people are saying. It will be easier to hear from you than to overhear at the water cooler. In telling her, however, you should reassure her that it is just a few men who obviously feel so threatened by her success that they have to deride it somehow and that she shouldn't let it upset her because no one is paying any attention to them anyway.

Q. *One of the executives in my company is forever touching me, complimenting me, and suggesting that we get together outside the office. This is extremely annoy-*

ing, and I am not sure how to get him to stop without being rude myself. What should I do?

A. Sexual harassment in the office is nothing new and has been the subject of many magazine articles and lawsuits, but that doesn't make it any more comfortable to be the object of unwanted sexual attentions. First, make it clear to this man that you appreciate him as a business associate but that you do not appreciate his sexual advances. Say, "Steve, I really enjoy working with you and feel we make a good team, but it has to be all business. I don't appreciate your innuendos. I take my job seriously, as you do, and I expect to be treated as the professional person I feel I am."

If your good manners don't work and he continues to harass you, speak to your supervisor. If your boss is the guilty one, then speak to his boss. Have specific dates and times at hand and examples of exactly what was said and done. Write it in a memo, keeping a copy for yourself.

If this does nothing to stop the harassment, then go to the personnel director with a copy of the memo and any new documentation. The personnel director should intercede for you and is in a position to warn or even fire the offender or to file a legal complaint. If the personnel director or department does nothing, then you have the legal right to do so yourself, filing a complaint with your area Equal Employment Opportunities Commission.

Q. *Although most of the men in my office are pretty used to women co-workers by now, they still fall back into patterns of expecting women to do "the women's work" in the office. I don't even think they are aware of it, but at every meeting, they expect me to pour the coffee, refill their cups, and take the notes. How can I get them to change this without making a big deal out of it or appearing hostile?*

A. First, don't sit near the coffee pot. Second, when a man tries to catch your eye with that coffee glint in his, become very busy with your papers. If he actually asks you to get him a cup of coffee, say, "I'm really busy right now—perhaps you or Andrew can do it," or, "You're closer to the pot, James; it will be easier for you—and while you're there, I could use a refill, too! Thanks so much."

If you run into men who still consider a woman the only one eligible for taking notes at a meeting, you can follow the same procedure. Say, "Suppose someone else takes the notes this time—I took them at the last three meetings." They should get the message. If asked again at the next meeting, say gently and with a smile, "It's not my turn yet—there are quite a few other people who haven't served as note-taker before the responsibility goes back to me."

This is not to mean that you never take a turn or that you don't ask the person next to you if he would like a cup of coffee if you are getting yourself one. Always offer to take a turn once it is established that those jobs are shared equally.

Q. *I am the only woman in an office of men. They socialize outside the office but have never invited me to* *join them, nor have they invited my husband and me when they get together with their wives in groups for dinner. We all work well together and have developed good professional friendships, so I do not take it personally that they don't like me but that they just haven't thought of including me. How can I change this?*

A. If you have the interest, time, and energy for joining them for a drink after work, say so. Tell them you are all a team, and you would like to discuss the day's events with them when they go out. They can hardly say no and will likely think to include you in the future.

In the same fashion, make the first move to include yourself in their gatherings with spouses by inviting them and their wives to dinner at your home. After being entertained by you, most will reciprocate by including you and your husband the next time they are entertaining the group.

Especially for Men

Q. *I am a junior executive in my company. When I am seated at my desk and someone enters, should I rise? Are there any guidelines for when I should stand?*
A. You should stand for:

- An executive, male or female, of higher rank than yours
- A male client
- A female client
- A female executive at your level, unless she is in and out of your office frequently

There is no need to stand for your secretary or assistant, whether male or female.

Q. *Should men stand when a woman enters or leaves a conference room?*
A. Only the man seated in the chair next to her rises, to pull out her chair. Other men in the room remain seated.

Q. *Should men hold or open doors for women in a business surrounding?*
A. There are times when social manners carry over into business situations, and this is one of them. Yes,

men should extend this courtesy, unless the woman with them objects. It should not be an issue—even if the woman expects to have the door opened for her, she should not stand at the door waiting for a business associate to maneuver around her to reach for the handle, since she is perfectly capable of opening it herself.

Q. *Should men stand aside and let women off elevators first in an office building?*
A. No. The people closest to the door exit when the door opens, whether men or women. Either one would extend the courtesy of holding the door if the elevator were crowded and there were several people exiting.

Q. *Should men remove their hats in elevators in office buildings?*
A. No, this is a time when social manners do not extend to the office. He may keep his hat on until he gets to his office.

Q. *I am a male secretary to a woman executive. Occasionally we go to lunch together to discuss business problems. Should I pay the bill on those occasions?*
A. No, she pays, just as a male executive would. There are some situations when a junior member, in the company of a senior executive, either male or female, picks up the check at the suggestion of his boss, since the executive has approval over his expense account and would rather allocate the amount in this way. Otherwise, it is customary for the higher-

ranking person, who has issued the luncheon invitation, to pay the bill.

Q. *A group of young (unmarried) executives in our office like to go out after work occasionally for a beer or a cocktail. We have not included the two female executives because the talk gets pretty rough sometimes and it doesn't seem appropriate. We hear that they resent not being included. How should we handle it?*

A. Invite the women to join you from time to time. If the talk is too rough for them, they will either say so or decline the invitation in the future. You all might decide, as well, that you could manage a conversation after work that didn't include inappropriate language, if you feel the way you speak would be alarming or upsetting to newcomers to your social group.

Q. *When approaching a revolving door, should the man or the woman go first?*

A. Based solely on average physical strength, the man should go first, since revolving doors that are not already turning can sometimes be difficult to maneuver.

Q. *When our company entertains clients socially, do I use business manners or social manners?*

A. Even though the event (dinner, theater, opera, etc.) has been arranged for business reasons, the manners used are social ones. In these cases, a man opens doors for a woman, hangs up her coat, stands when she enters the room and remains standing until she is seated, serves her before himself, has her precede him behind a maître d' or into a taxi, assists her into her coat, and removes his hat in the elevator. Social manners, like business manners, are an asset for a smart businessman. Being able to use whichever the occasion calls for is to his advantage in business, showing those senior to him that he can handle himself in any situation.

Q. *I have always considered myself as a true equal opportunity employer and have hired and promoted women to executive positions for years because they were the most qualified for the job. However, I have noticed that they are sometimes offended by something I do or say. Are there any pitfalls which I should watch out for?*

A. Yes, there are. Old traditions sometimes creep in accidentally and unintentionally, which take the equality out of many employment situations.

- Don't call women in the office by pet names. "Honey," "Sweetie," and "Dear" are not professional titles. It is likely that you do not call men by those names.
- Don't call a female secretary your "girl." She has a name. Refer to her as "Susan, my secretary," with those who do not know her name and as "Susan" (or "Ms Goldwyn" if titles are used in the office) with those in the office who know who she is. Unless you have high school workers in your office, the female members of your staff are always women not girls.
- Don't assume that just because an associate or

employee is a woman she should make, buy, or deliver your coffee every day. She was not hired as your personal servant. Assuming all your parts are working, you are capable of getting your own coffee. Go a step further and get her a cup every now and then until you have established a new partnership of thoughtfulness and cooperation where whoever is nearest the coffee pot offers a cup to the other.

· In executive meetings, don't assign note-taking chores only to women because they have been traditional stenographers in the past. Men are perfectly capable of taking notes, and there is no reason not to share the responsibility equally among your male and female executives.

· Don't touch the women in your office. However warm and friendly the gesture, it can be misinterpreted as sexual harassment only because so many men use touch in that way. Certainly shake hands, as you would with male associates but leave physical contact at that.

· Don't refer to the women in your office by their appearance, as in "The prettiest operations manager we have ever had." Surely it would never have occurred to you to refer to her predecessor as "handsome."

Index

About the Author

Elizabeth L. Post, granddaughter-in-law of the legendary Emily Post, has earned the mantle of her predecessor as America's foremost authority on etiquette. Mrs. Post has revised the classic *Etiquette* four times since 1965, and has written *Emily Post's Complete Book of Wedding Etiquette; Emily Post's Wedding Planner; Please, Say Please; The Complete Book of Entertaining* with co-author Anthony Staffieri; *Emily Post Talks with Teens* with co-author Joan M. Coles; along with other titles in this series of question-and-answer books: *Emily Post on Etiquette, Emily Post on Entertaining, Emily Post on Weddings,* and *Emily Post on Invitations and Letters.* Mrs. Post's advice on etiquette may also be found in the monthly column she writes for *Good Housekeeping* magazine, "Etiquette for Every Day."

Mrs. Post and her husband, William, divide their time between homes in Florida and Vermont.